Complete Horoscope

Cancer 2024

Monthly astrological forecasts for 2024

TATIANA BORSCH

Copyright © 2023 Tatiana Borsch.

All rights reserved. No part of this book may be reproduced, stored, or transmitted by any means—whether auditory, graphic, mechanical, or electronic—without written permission of the author, except in the case of brief excerpts used in critical articles and reviews. Unauthorized reproduction of any part of this work is illegal and is punishable by law.

Because of the dynamic nature of the Internet, any web addresses or links contained in this book may have changed since publication and may no longer be valid. The views expressed in this work are solely those of the author and do not necessarily reflect the views of the publisher, and the publisher hereby disclaims any responsibility for them.

This book is a work of non-fiction. Unless otherwise noted, the author and the publisher make no explicit guarantees as to the accuracy of the information contained in this book and in some cases, names of people and places have been altered to protect their privacy.

Any people depicted in stock imagery provided by Getty Images are models, and such images are being used for illustrative purposes only. Certain stock imagery © Getty Images.

Translated from Russian by Sonja Swenson
Translation copyright © Coinflow Limited, Cyprus
AstraArt Books is an imprint of Coinflow limited, Cyprus
Published by Coinflow Limited, Cyprus

For queries please contact: tatianaborsch@yahoo.com
ISBN 978-9925-609-48-2 (paperback)
ISBN 978-9925-609-49-9 (ebook)

Contents

General Astrological Forecast for 2024 5

2024 Overview for Cancer 11

January 14

February 17

March 20

April 23

May 26

June 29

July 32

August 35

September 38

October 41

November 44

December 47

Cancer Description 50

A Guide to The Moon Cycle and Lunar Days 55

A Guide to Zodiac Compatibility 84

Love Description of Zodiac Signs 92

General Astrological Forecast for 2024

We are embarking on yet another difficult year, which can generally be divided into two very different periods. During the first half of the year, Jupiter, which is the most powerful planet in our solar system, will be in the sign of Taurus, creating a favorable aspect with Saturn. That means that both peoples' lives and events on the political stage will play out rather predictably.

This is a very good time for China – it will continue to expand its power, both economically and politically, which will of course impact its position in the global arena. We might see successful negotiations regarding Taiwan.

The first half of 2024 will also be very positive for India. Its economy is surging – over the next three to four years, it will be able to make significant investments in resolving problems such as poverty and develop its infrastructure and industry. It will become a global economic leader.

However, things are not so rosy in the Old World – Europe, where economic drivers such as Germany, are going through a troublesome astrological period. In India, this is known as Sade Sati (Saturn's transit through the sign of the Moon, which often includes the Moon's neighboring zodiac sign). Usually, this period lasts about three years. Each country will experience things its own way. For Germany, this most likely means an economic slowdown and domestic political and social turbulence. This is a trend that began in 2022 and will last for about three years.

The first half of 2024 is crucial for Russia, as presidential elections will take place in 2024. I predict that Putin will remain in power, despite the Russian opposition and meddling from the West, which will be unprecedented this time. Though Putin will remain in the Kremlin, his government will see a lot of turnover, as will other power structures.

The war in Ukraine will begin to slow down somewhat during the first half of the year, and though there will not be any major hostilities, skirmishes will break out in various spots on various fronts.

Ukraine's difficulties began with the Sade Sati in 2020. In 2024-2025, we will see this phenomenon reach its final phase. I believe that there is a very high chance of the country being divided into spheres of influence, with its very independence jeopardized. In 2024, and perhaps somewhat sooner, Poland might openly lay claim to Lviv and the western territories that were ceded to Ukraine following World War Two.

With regard to Ukraine's territories currently under Russian occupation – we will see a continuation of major construction and infrastructure restoration. I believe that in the first half of 2024, Russia's expansion may continue, as other Russian-speaking regions of Ukraine fall under its influence. May 2024 might be a very important time for this.

Economically, this is a hard time for Russia. Sanctions and trade limitations will make things significantly more difficult. There may not be enough budget for military operations, along with economic development, and major construction in the regions now impacted by war. But in the end, there will be an acceptable balance. Russia's economic recovery will be active enough, and as a result, we might see new companies created in regions around the country.

A major astrological event will take place from April 18-26, 2024. Two giants of the solar system – Jupiter and Uranus – will be in conjunction. This is one of the most unusual unions when it comes to finances. Depending on individual horoscopes, some people might see significant achievements here, while others will see unexpected changes for the worse. In principle, this is a neutral-positive aspect, but everything depends on individual information. This is an interesting time for cryptocurrency – we might see significant ups and downs with new financial instruments, which will seriously alter the currency markets, as Uranus in Taurus will lead to many financial shifts.

But also remember that during this time, we may see positive business propositions, career changes, promotions, salary raises, and successful investments!

In 2024, all businesses related to agriculture and produce might develop rapidly. More people might be noticeably more focused on eating a healthy diet.

The second half of 2024 will be much more troublesome for all countries, and far more difficult than the first half.

On May 25, Jupiter will transit to Gemini, and by June, we might start to see changes in plans and conflicts drag out, both in our interpersonal relationships and between countries. By mid-August, Jupiter will be forming a harsh aspect with Saturn, which promises a battle between old structures and the new world we live in. This aspect will repeat again in the fall and winter of 2024. Our world abounds with contradictions, and this will only become more apparent. The economic crisis will worsen, and almost no country will be spared.

The war in Ukraine will gain momentum once again. In the fall and winter of 2024, things will become difficult for Russia, as the hostilities take on a new intensity. This will continue into the first half of 2025, though gradually it will become clear that there is no military solution to this conflict, and things will start to die down. Sanctions will remain in place, though slowly but surely, things will head in a more constructive direction.

During the second half of the year, the European Union will see division among its member states. This trend will continue into 2025 as well. We might see some countries moving toward greater independence from Brussels. The reason may be the economic crisis, which will force many governments to work on behalf of their own countries. Obviously we won't see any repeats of Brexit in 2024, though this may appear somewhat later. Over the next three to four years, the EU will undergo serious changes, and the European Commission might lose some of its powers, as dictating the rules of the game to the world will become much more difficult.

With regard to the United States, 2024 might be particularly difficult. Pluto is returning to its position in the US birth chart, and this is very important, as it will be in the sector of the sky responsible for the banking system, finances, and even society's emotional state.

Pluto is the planet responsible for purification and renewal, but it also brings the destruction of anything obsolete, which may trigger global crises, which are inevitable with any change in the system. That is why in 2024, economic strife may trigger demonstrations against the current government, as well as a serious struggle for power among members of the ruling class.

During the second half of the year, the United States may lose a lot of allies – this trend will continue into 2025. Perhaps this will be due to a stronger China, Russia, and India, or alternatively, growing economic problems. The US will weaken in its role as the hegemon.

The US presidential elections in 2024 may bring a repeat of what we saw in 2020. It is hard to imagine Joe Biden hanging onto the presidency. He will leave. But these elections will be full of scandal, most likely due to Trump's bombastic speeches.

During the second half of the year, Jupiter will be in Gemini, which supports Trump, as he himself is a Gemini. During the first half of the year, however, despite his histrionics, Trump will spend the first half of 2024 busy with legal troubles that began in 2023. But during the second half of the year, he will be at the center of society's attention – what more could a politician need? Both Trump and Ron de Santis have a good shot at the presidency. De Santis's birth time is unknown, but I think he has a good chance.

Another thorn in the US's side may be the situation in the Middle East, which is already unstable, but in 2024, some kind of military confrontation may break out.

Jupiter in Gemini creates a negative aspect with Saturn, which will close in mid-August, and which portends difficulties for the global economy. This means a situation that is highly unstable, with volatile markets and trouble in the banking sector.

We might, however, see scientific breakthroughs – perhaps new technology and discoveries await in the hands of the world's young and talented scientists.

Fashion will become more feminine and elegant during the first half of the year. Jupiter in Taurus means that we can expect more fitted silhouettes, and perhaps greater focus on traditional garb. Beige will be the color of the day, as will all hues of gold and brown. As always, black will be in demand. Clothing will be monochromatic.

During the second half of the year, we can expect light and dark blue, green, and unusual color combinations. The look will be unkempt and carefree, with a greater focus on youth fashions than the classics. Jupiter in Gemini also suggests flowing, translucent fabrics.

All year long, the weather will be unstable, with flooding affecting coastal countries and islands. We might see a more serious version of what has already happened in several regions of the world. During the second half of the year, many countries can expect to deal with strong winds and tornadoes.

While we can say that everyone has their own fate, global circumstances often are indirectly reflected in each of our lives.

Despite all the ups and downs, the first half of 2024 is the best time for getting married, having babies, or buying real estate.

During the second half of the year, I would not recommend any long-distance travel, starting any legal proceedings, or making important decisions about moving. During this time, many relationships will fall apart, if things were already on the rocks. But you can find out more about that in my forecast for each Zodiac sign.

Best of luck in 2024!

Astrologist Tatiana Borsch

2024 Overview for Cancer

2024 is a watershed for you, as you move from the past into the future. This is a year of harvesting what you deserve. You will reap what you have sown, no more, and no less.

Work

During the first half of the year, things will be going your way. You will be surrounded by friends, like-minded people, and those with influence and power. Thanks to their help, you will seriously shore up your position at work, and even become fairly well-known in your field.

Your contacts with business partners in other cities or abroad will also develop nicely, and you might reconnect with former associates or spend a lot of time traveling.

Employees can count on a promotion, which will go hand in hand with greater influence and possibly even a raise.

Those who work in the creative fields are in for particular success. This includes actors, musicians, artists, and anyone who works with words. They will see their popularity grow, as well as their income.

This winning streak might reach a crescendo in May. In March and April, you will be pleased with the way things are going.

During the second half of the year, things will become more difficult. Starting in June, you will see changes for the worse, and all Cancers will experience this differently.

Business owners and managers will have to deal with audits, a resurgence of old legal troubles, and all of this might take on a highly unpredictable hue.

You will not be able to resolve all of these difficulties in 2024, and some of them will continue into 2025.

Your relationship with colleagues in other cities or abroad will also become significantly more complex after June, and some business partners far away might begin behaving irresponsibly or even with hostilities. Alternatively, difficulties on the world stage will throw a monkey wrench into your cooperation.

Money

During the first half of 2024, your finances are looking stable, but things will take a turn. You will spend more than you make, so many Cancers will need to keep an eye on their bank accounts. But it is always darkest before dawn, and you are sure to recover by the second half of 2025.

Love and family

During the first half of the year, things will be peaceful, and loving couples will live together in harmony. Your children will be a source of joy, though you may spend the lion's share of the family budget on their needs.

You might get back in touch with old friends or a former flame. They may live far away now, or perhaps a little closer to home.

Single Cancers will have an excellent opportunity to meet a new partner, and that will probably happen among friends, while traveling, or among people from somewhere far away.

During the second half of 2024, that is, from June to December, expect a lot of psychological and emotional turbulence.

During this time, your relationships may grow more complicated, and you are not the culprit here. You may experience serious trouble involving relatives and gossip, and it will be difficult to see who is in the right and who is in the wrong.

This unpleasant trend will take place from August to December. In order to not let it spoil your life, hold onto your loved one and remember that the most important thing in life is love and family, and we can and must simply get through the rest.

Health

During the first half of the year, you are healthy, energetic, and leave great impressions on everyone Fate sends your way. After June, you will be more sluggish, and old chronic diseases may become aggravated, or perhaps new ones will appear. Be careful when driving and traveling, especially in August and December!

January

New York Time			London Time		
Calendar Day	Lunar Day	Lunar Day Start Time	Calendar Day	Lunar Day	Lunar Day Start Time
01/01/24	21	10.18 PM	01/01/24	21	10.02 PM
02/01/24	22	11.16 PM	02/01/24	22	11.08 PM
04/01/24	23	12.14 AM	04/01/24	23	12.14 AM
05/01/24	24	1.14 AM	05/01/24	24	1.22 AM
06/01/24	25	2.16 AM	06/01/24	25	2.32 AM
07/01/24	26	3.20 AM	07/01/24	26	3.44 AM
08/01/24	27	4.26 AM	08/01/24	27	4.57 AM
09/01/24	28	5.30 AM	09/01/24	28	6.07 AM
10/01/24	29	6.31 AM	10/01/24	29	7.10 AM
11/01/24	1	6.58 AM	11/01/24	30	8.03 AM
11/01/24	2	7.26 AM	11/01/24	1	11.58 AM
12/01/24	3	8.13 AM	12/01/24	2	8.44 AM
13/01/24	4	8.53 AM	13/01/24	3	9.16 AM
14/01/24	5	9.27 AM	14/01/24	4	9.42 AM
15/01/24	6	9.59 AM	15/01/24	5	10.05 AM
16/01/24	7	10.29 AM	16/01/24	6	10.25 AM
17/01/24	8	10.58 AM	17/01/24	7	10.45 AM
18/01/24	9	11.29 AM	18/01/24	8	11.07 AM
19/01/24	10	12.04 PM	19/01/24	9	11.32 AM
20/01/24	11	12.42 PM	20/01/24	10	12.02 PM
21/01/24	12	1.26 PM	21/01/24	11	12.39 PM
22/01/24	13	2.16 PM	22/01/24	12	1.25 PM
23/01/24	14	3.11 PM	23/01/24	13	2.19 PM
24/01/24	15	4.10 PM	24/01/24	14	3.21 PM
25/01/24	16	5.10 PM	25/01/24	15	4.27 PM
26/01/24	17	6.10 PM	26/01/24	16	5.35 PM
27/01/24	18	7.10 PM	27/01/24	17	6.43 PM
28/01/24	19	8.08 PM	28/01/24	18	7.50 PM
29/01/24	20	9.06 PM	29/01/24	19	8.56 PM
30/01/24	21	10.04 PM	30/01/24	20	10.01 PM
31/01/24	22	11.02 PM	31/01/24	21	11.08 PM

You can find the description of each lunar day in the chapter "A Guide to The Moon Cycle and Lunar Days"

January is a great time to strengthen your relationship with your environment and seek support from the right people. A friend in court is better than a penny in purse.

Work

After the holidays are over, Cancers can expect to focus on work instead, and resolving old problems.

This may include legal issues, or possibly something involving colleagues from other cities or abroad. The first 10 days of the month will be the rockiest. Things will start looking up during the latter part of the month, and you can expect help from a friend or someone in a position of influence, who will support you in both words and deeds, or might act as an intermediary. Thanks to your shared efforts, things will be safely resolved by the end of the month.

Many Cancers will meet someone influential or powerful. Their help will prove to be swift, effective, and timely. If they want to go into business together, the stars recommend you accept the offer, after carefully reviewing all of the documents and any financial risks.

Money

Your bank account is looking stable, but that is it. Your income is modest, but your expenses are reasonable and predictable. Many will have to pay back old debts, and in this regard, the entire month, especially the first 10 days, will be somewhat challenging.

Love and family

January is a great time for strengthening your business relations, as well as making romantic connections. You might Mr. or Ms. Right, and you will not be disappointed later on.

After a long period of turbulence in your personal life, which many Cancers have gone through, the stars will shift from anger to mercy, sending new people and opportunities your way. The best time for this is after January 11.

This is not a bad time for relationships with family and others, especially if there are no financial claims at stake.

Be careful when traveling in January, because things may not turn out as you had hoped.

This is especially true for any travel abroad, where you may run into all kinds of obstacles.

Health

For most of January, you are feeling energetic, and you have no reason to fear falling ill. From the 22nd to 31st, the stars recommend you take it easy and focus on yourself. During this time, you might expect periods of fatigue, lethargy, or colds, and chronic conditions may exacerbate.

February

New York Time			London Time		
Calendar Day	Lunar Day	Lunar Day Start Time	Calendar Day	Lunar Day	Lunar Day Start Time
02/02/24	23	12.02 AM	02/02/24	22	12.16 AM
03/02/24	24	1.04 AM	03/02/24	23	1.25 AM
04/02/24	25	2.07 AM	04/02/24	24	2.36 AM
05/02/24	26	3.11 AM	05/02/24	25	3.46 AM
06/02/24	27	4.12 AM	06/02/24	26	4.51 AM
07/02/24	28	5.10 AM	07/02/24	27	5.48 AM
08/02/24	29	6.00 AM	08/02/24	28	6.35 AM
09/02/24	30	6.44 AM	09/02/24	29	7.12 AM
09/02/24	1	6.00 PM	09/02/24	1	11.00 PM
10/02/24	2	7.22 AM	10/02/24	2	7.41 AM
11/02/24	3	7.56 AM	11/02/24	3	8.06 AM
12/02/24	4	8.28 AM	12/02/24	4	8.28 AM
13/02/24	5	8.59 AM	13/02/24	5	8.49 AM
14/02/24	6	9.30 AM	14/02/24	6	9.11 AM
15/02/24	7	10.04 AM	15/02/24	7	9.36 AM
16/02/24	8	10.42 AM	16/02/24	8	10.05 AM
17/02/24	9	11.25 AM	17/02/24	9	10.39 AM
18/02/24	10	12.13 PM	18/02/24	10	11.22 AM
19/02/24	11	1.06 PM	19/02/24	11	12.14 PM
20/02/24	12	2.03 PM	20/02/24	12	1.13 PM
21/02/24	13	3.03 PM	21/02/24	13	2.18 PM
22/02/24	14	4.03 PM	22/02/24	14	3.25 PM
23/02/24	15	5.02 PM	23/02/24	15	4.32 PM
24/02/24	16	6.01 PM	24/02/24	16	5.39 PM
25/02/24	17	6.59 PM	25/02/24	17	6.45 PM
26/02/24	18	7.57 PM	26/02/24	18	7.51 PM
27/02/24	19	8.55 PM	27/02/24	19	8.57 PM
28/02/24	20	9.54 PM	28/02/24	20	10.04 PM
29/02/24	21	10.54 PM	29/02/24	21	11.13 PM

You can find the description of each lunar day in the chapter "A Guide to The Moon Cycle and Lunar Days"

After a successful January, you will start to see that your luck and energy are beginning to wane. February will require both restraint and discretion in all areas of your life, from the romantic to the diplomatic.

Work

Cancers who are part of the working world would do well to concentrate on the projects that are already in motion and not start anything big right now.

Your main problem this month might be a relationship with someone around you, especially when it comes to finance. You might have a disagreement with friends or someone who provided you with some kind of service recently, and probably over debt, money, or some other tangible asset. It's entirely possible these claims are justified, and you will have to pay what you owe.

Your relationship with colleagues in other cities or abroad is moving along nicely, and you might take a trip or start organizing one.

Employees will have an opportunity to take some time off and head somewhere far away, or maybe just to your family's cabin. Take advantage of a chance like this, because life doesn't revolve around work, and you can take some time away from the office. What's more, nothing major is happening right now, anyway.

Money

Your bank account is less than stable right now.

You will be spending constantly, as many Cancers are repaying their debts, settling credit, or perhaps facing unexpected home expenses. Get ready for February ahead of time, so that you aren't caught off guard.

You may have less income than usual, and things will only improve after March, so keep an eye on your budget and try to cut out any unnecessary spending.

Love and family

Your romantic and family relationships are looking rather stormy. Misunderstandings and arguments might set the backdrop for the entire month, perhaps over unresolved financial issues, or possibly clashing worldviews or even differing value systems. Can you get through it? Yes! The stars predict that if your love is strong, you will have the strength to overcome any obstacle.

If this is a recent romance, be careful, though. February will reveal your partner's true colors. That is, you will have a moment of truth, and it's always better to know for sure.

Any trips planned this month will go well, though you will find yourself spending a lot of money.

Health

In February, you are not feeling very energetic, and you might have bouts of fatigue, sluggishness, or even depression.

If you are elderly or weakened in any way, chronic conditions are likely to return, and it's worth heading them off right away. The stars suggest taking care of your body and avoiding any colds, infections or other dangerous situations.

March

New York Time			London Time		
Calendar Day	Lunar Day	Lunar Day Start Time	Calendar Day	Lunar Day	Lunar Day Start Time
01/03/24	22	11.56 PM	02/03/24	22	12.22 AM
03/03/24	23	12.57 AM	03/03/24	23	1.30 AM
04/03/24	24	1.58 AM	04/03/24	24	2.36 AM
05/03/24	25	2.55 AM	05/03/24	25	3.35 AM
06/03/24	26	3.48 AM	06/03/24	26	4.25 AM
07/03/24	27	4.34 AM	07/03/24	27	5.05 AM
08/03/24	28	5.14 AM	08/03/24	28	5.38 AM
09/03/24	29	5.50 AM	09/03/24	29	6.05 AM
10/03/24	1	4.02 AM	10/03/24	30	6.28 AM
10/03/24	2	6.23 AM	10/03/24	1	9.02 AM
11/03/24	3	6.55 AM	11/03/24	2	6.50 AM
12/03/24	4	7.27 AM	12/03/24	3	7.12 AM
13/03/24	5	8.01 AM	13/03/24	4	7.36 AM
14/03/24	6	8.38 AM	14/03/24	5	8.04 AM
15/03/24	7	9.21 AM	15/03/24	6	8.37 AM
16/03/24	8	10.08 AM	16/03/24	7	9.19 AM
17/03/24	9	11.01 AM	17/03/24	8	10.08 AM
18/03/24	10	11.57 AM	18/03/24	9	11.06 AM
19/03/24	11	12.56 PM	19/03/24	10	12.09 PM
20/03/24	12	1.56 PM	20/03/24	11	1.16 PM
21/03/24	13	2.55 PM	21/03/24	12	2.23 PM
22/03/24	14	3.54 PM	22/03/24	13	3.30 PM
23/03/24	15	4.52 PM	23/03/24	14	4.36 PM
24/03/24	16	5.50 PM	24/03/24	15	5.42 PM
25/03/24	17	6.48 PM	25/03/24	16	6.48 PM
26/03/24	18	7.47 PM	26/03/24	17	7.55 PM
27/03/24	19	8.47 PM	27/03/24	18	9.03 PM
28/03/24	20	9.48 PM	28/03/24	19	10.12 PM
29/03/24	21	10.50 PM	29/03/24	20	11.21 PM
30/03/24	22	11.50 PM	31/03/24	21	12.27 AM

You can find the description of each lunar day in the chapter "A Guide to The Moon Cycle and Lunar Days"

After a murky, troubling February, March looks more positive and more interesting, as well. Life is going back to normal, so go for it!

Work

You can divide March into three distinct periods. The first 10 days is a good time to work on your relationship with colleagues in other cities or abroad, or even take a trip. During this time, you might meet new business partners or someone influential who might open new doors.

After March 10, you will be fairly busy, but financial matters will become a sore spot. You may need to settle old debts, or alternatively, fulfill obligations you took on earlier. You might clash with someone over material issues, which is especially likely if you have differing viewpoints on money or other tangible assets.

For the last 10 days of the month, things will be much more positive. You will be able to settle any delicate issues and things will start moving along quickly.

Money

Financially, March is not a great time for you. You won't end up penniless, but you will be bleeding money this month.

Many Cancers will have to settle old debts or close out credits, or otherwise handle matters related to earlier obligations.

Expect to spend the most from March 7 to 10, but you can expect a healthy sum to come in during the last 10 days of the month.

Love and family

Those who are more focused on personal matters will also run into money trouble this month. That may be due to expenses related to travel, which is highly likely during the first 10 days of March. Alternatively, it may be due to a conflict with friends or a group of people who may demand you settle old debts.

Financial issues may mar things for couples, whether they are married or not, but here, things may also depend on your real feelings and both parties' intentions. If you aren't stingy, you will manage to avoid the very worst.

Many Cancers will be running into old friends, and your relationship with them will develop very nicely.

That is especially the case for friends living in different cities or countries, as well as relatives.

Health

In March, you are feeling noticeably more energetic, and have no reason to fear falling ill.

April

New York Time			London Time		
Calendar Day	Lunar Day	Lunar Day Start Time	Calendar Day	Lunar Day	Lunar Day Start Time
01/04/24	23	12.48 AM	01/04/24	22	2.27 AM
02/04/24	24	1.40 AM	02/04/24	23	3.19 AM
03/04/24	25	2.27 AM	03/04/24	24	4.02 AM
04/04/24	26	3.08 AM	04/04/24	25	4.36 AM
05/04/24	27	3.44 AM	05/04/24	26	5.04 AM
06/04/24	28	4.18 AM	06/04/24	27	5.28 AM
07/04/24	29	4.49 AM	07/04/24	28	5.50 AM
08/04/24	30	5.21 AM	08/04/24	29	6.12 AM
08/04/24	1	2.23 PM	08/04/24	1	7.23 PM
09/04/24	2	6.54 AM	09/04/24	2	6.35 AM
10/04/24	3	7.31 AM	10/04/24	3	7.01 AM
11/04/24	4	8.12 AM	11/04/24	4	7.32 AM
12/04/24	5	8.58 AM	12/04/24	5	8.11 AM
13/04/24	6	9.50 AM	13/04/24	6	8.58 AM
14/04/24	7	10.47 AM	14/04/24	7	9.55 AM
15/04/24	8	11.47 AM	15/04/24	8	10.58 AM
16/04/24	9	12.47 PM	16/04/24	9	12.04 PM
17/04/24	10	1.47 PM	17/04/24	10	1.12 PM
18/04/24	11	2.46 PM	18/04/24	11	2.19 PM
19/04/24	12	3.45 PM	19/04/24	12	3.26 PM
20/04/24	13	4.43 PM	20/04/24	13	4.32 PM
21/04/24	14	5.41 PM	21/04/24	14	5.38 PM
22/04/24	15	6.40 PM	22/04/24	15	6.45 PM
23/04/24	16	7.40 PM	23/04/24	16	7.53 PM
24/04/24	17	8.41 PM	24/04/24	17	9.02 PM
25/04/24	18	9.43 PM	25/04/24	18	10.12 PM
26/04/24	19	10.45 PM	26/04/24	19	11.20 PM
27/04/24	20	11.43 PM	28/04/24	20	12.22 AM
29/04/24	21	12.37 AM	29/04/24	21	1.17 AM
30/04/24	22	1.25 AM	30/04/24	22	2.02 AM

You can find the description of each lunar day in the chapter "A Guide to The Moon Cycle and Lunar Days"

You may have won the battle, but that doesn't mean the war is over. In April, you will once again have to reexamine your goals and make some necessary changes.

Work

April is a busy month for you, but also a time for anxiety and general fussiness. You might be involved in negotiations with colleagues from other cities or abroad, who will drag things out, but closer to May, you will come to a positive result. You may also even take a productive trip during this time.

Business owners and managers might finish up previous projects and make changes to whatever is standing in your way. Your friends or someone influential may play an important role this month. This time, their influence will be positive.

Any problems from earlier months have already been resolved, and things are looking calmer, now.

Employees might spend a lot of time discussing their responsibilities or a new title with management, and by late April or perhaps the first half of May, you will get your way.

Money

Financially, this month is not a bad time for you. You will have money coming in regularly, and somewhat more than usual.

Expect to receive the largest sums on April 8, 9, 16-18, 26, and 27.

Your expenses are low, and most will take place during the last 10 days of the month.

Love and family

Your personal life will be on the back burner this month, as you will be so focused on work during the first 20 days of April. For this reason, your relationship with your partner or spouse might cool a bit. In order to avoid trouble here, try to take the time to explain to your better half why you are so busy, and you will be pleased with their response.

Things will change a bit during the last 10 days of April. Here, you will have an opportunity to spend more time with friends and loved ones and to attend more events and generally be more present in your own life.

You might see people from your past such as old friends, and perhaps even an old flame. This encounter will be both pleasant and useful to you.

However, if you meet anyone new while Mercury is in retrograde from April 2-25, this encounter may prove superficial and unreliable, so don't place too much stock in them.

Health

In April, your body is at its very peak and any illnesses will pass you by.

May

	New York Time			London Time	
Calendar Day	Lunar Day	Lunar Day Start Time	Calendar Day	Lunar Day	Lunar Day Start Time
01/05/24	23	2.07 AM	01/05/24	23	2.38 AM
02/05/24	24	2.43 AM	02/05/24	24	3.07 AM
03/05/24	25	3.16 AM	03/05/24	25	3.31 AM
04/05/24	26	3.47 AM	04/05/24	26	3.53 AM
05/05/24	27	4.18 AM	05/05/24	27	4.14 AM
06/05/24	28	4.49 AM	06/05/24	28	4.35 AM
07/05/24	29	5.23 AM	07/05/24	29	4.59 AM
07/05/24	1	11.24 PM	08/05/24	1	4.24 AM
08/05/24	2	6.02 AM	08/05/24	2	5.27 AM
09/05/24	3	6.46 AM	09/05/24	3	6.02 AM
10/05/24	4	7.36 AM	10/05/24	4	6.46 AM
11/05/24	5	8.33 AM	11/05/24	5	7.39 AM
12/05/24	6	9.33 AM	12/05/24	6	8.41 AM
13/05/24	7	10.34 AM	13/05/24	7	9.48 AM
14/05/24	8	11.36 AM	14/05/24	8	10.57 AM
15/05/24	9	12.36 PM	15/05/24	9	12.06 PM
16/05/24	10	1.35 PM	16/05/24	10	1.13 PM
17/05/24	11	2.33 PM	17/05/24	11	2.19 PM
18/05/24	12	3.31 PM	18/05/24	12	3.25 PM
19/05/24	13	4.29 PM	19/05/24	13	4.32 PM
20/05/24	14	5.29 PM	20/05/24	14	5.39 PM
21/05/24	15	6.31 PM	21/05/24	15	6.49 PM
22/05/24	16	7.33 PM	22/05/24	16	7.59 PM
23/05/24	17	8.36 PM	23/05/24	17	9.09 PM
24/05/24	18	9.37 PM	24/05/24	18	10.15 PM
25/05/24	19	10.33 PM	25/05/24	19	11.13 PM
26/05/24	20	11.24 PM	27/05/24	20	12.02 AM
28/05/24	21	12.07 AM	28/05/24	21	12.40 AM
29/05/24	22	12.45 AM	29/05/24	22	1.11 AM
30/05/24	23	1.19 AM	30/05/24	23	1.36 AM
31/05/24	24	1.50 AM	31/05/24	24	1.58 AM

You can find the description of each lunar day in the chapter "A Guide to The Moon Cycle and Lunar Days"

You will remember most of May as an exciting, successful time. However, nothing is permanent, and this will be clear by the end of the month. Cinderella is leaving the ball and will have to take care of herself for a while.

Work

During the first 20 days of May, you will run into friends, business partners, and influential people. You might have intensive communication with colleagues in other cities or abroad, or even take a successful trip.

What's more, any further progress will require you to establish a firm foundation, which will keep you busy for the rest of the year.

Business owners and managers will be thinking about expanding their business and completing various tasks related to this meticulous endeavor. That will take place during different periods from 2024-2025, but by late May or early June, you are starting to transition to a new reality. It is not easy, but right now, you have no other choice.

Many Cancers will have to deal with unpleasant matters, as well. For example, past legal troubles may rear their ugly heads again. That will happen a little later, but it's worth bracing yourself for the inevitable now.

Money

Financially, May is full of ups and downs. You are spending almost as much as you earn, but there is reason to hope that by June, you will be back in the black.

Love and family

The best time for your personal life is the first 20 days of May. This is a great time for many Cancers to be busy with a variety of people, all of whom you love to be around.

You might get back in touch with old friends or someone from another city or abroad, or perhaps even take a successful trip.

During this period, single people and those who have been let down by past relationships might have an interesting encounter, which will bring some joy to their lives.

Even if your romance isn't for the long term (here, everything depends on your personal horoscope), it will give you life experience and happy memories.

Parents are pleased with their children, who are on a positive streak.

Though the first part of the month is a busy time full of activities, during the last 10 days, things will start to change. You will want to spend more time alone, or with loved ones, or perhaps setting up a home. The latter is a thing for the future, but you may be in the planning stages right now.

Health

For most of May, you are healthy, full of energy, and a social butterfly. After May 20, however, that will start to drop off.

Be very attentive to yourself if you are elderly or weakened, as you are embarking on a rather unfavorable time, when you may run into old illnesses or unexpected new ones, and this will last for the rest of the year.

June

New York Time			London Time		
Calendar Day	Lunar Day	Lunar Day Start Time	Calendar Day	Lunar Day	Lunar Day Start Time
01/06/24	25	2.19 AM	01/06/24	25	2.19 AM
02/06/24	26	2.49 AM	02/06/24	26	2.39 AM
03/06/24	27	3.21 AM	03/06/24	27	3.01 AM
04/06/24	28	3.56 AM	04/06/24	28	3.26 AM
05/06/24	29	4.37 AM	05/06/24	29	3.57 AM
06/06/24	30	5.24 AM	06/06/24	30	4.36 AM
06/06/24	1	8.40 AM	06/06/24	1	1.40 PM
07/06/24	2	6.18 AM	07/06/24	2	5.25 AM
08/06/24	3	7.17 AM	08/06/24	3	6.24 AM
09/06/24	4	8.19 AM	09/06/24	4	7.30 AM
10/06/24	5	9.22 AM	10/06/24	5	8.39 AM
11/06/24	6	10.23 AM	11/06/24	6	9.49 AM
12/06/24	7	11.23 AM	12/06/24	7	10.58 AM
13/06/24	8	12.22 PM	13/06/24	8	12.05 PM
14/06/24	9	1.20 PM	14/06/24	9	1.11 PM
15/06/24	10	2.18 PM	15/06/24	10	2.17 PM
16/06/24	11	3.17 PM	16/06/24	11	3.24 PM
17/06/24	12	4.17 PM	17/06/24	12	4.32 PM
18/06/24	13	5.19 PM	18/06/24	13	5.42 PM
19/06/24	14	6.22 PM	19/06/24	14	6.53 PM
20/06/24	15	7.25 PM	20/06/24	15	8.01 PM
21/06/24	16	8.24 PM	21/06/24	16	9.04 PM
22/06/24	17	9.18 PM	22/06/24	17	9.57 PM
23/06/24	18	10.06 PM	23/06/24	18	10.40 PM
24/06/24	19	10.46 PM	24/06/24	19	11.14 PM
25/06/24	20	11.22 PM	25/06/24	20	11.42 PM
26/06/24	21	11.53 PM	27/06/24	21	12.05 AM
28/06/24	22	12.23 AM	28/06/24	22	12.25 AM
29/06/24	23	12.52 AM	29/06/24	23	12.45 AM
30/06/24	24	1.23 AM	30/06/24	24	1.06 AM

You can find the description of each lunar day in the chapter "A Guide to The Moon Cycle and Lunar Days"

In June, you would be wise to keep your ambitions in check and remember that the more vigorously you strive to reach your goals, the harder you will make things for yourself. Slow and steady wins the race.

Work

Jupiter is shifting signs, which means abrupt changes in your situation. You will have less people around you, but more problems. Things will be quiet during the first 10 days of the month, but from June 9-19, expect a lot of challenges your way. Many Cancers will be dealing with past legal problems, or perhaps old debts or obligations will rear their ugly heads once again. You may even receive an unexpected visit from an auditing agency, so business owners and managers at every level need to be ready.

Employees would be wise to remember that their shortcomings and flaws will be more noticeable right now, and act accordingly.

You may deal with intrigue among colleagues and competition or come into undesirable information. Be very cautious and quiet during this difficult period.

Those with ties abroad will also face unpredictable situations. Slowly but surely, you will run into headwinds and even breakdowns starting around June 10, and don't expect any relief until after the 20th.

The last 10 days of the month will be calmer, and one way or another, your problems will start to resolve themselves, but that's no reason to let your guard down. Later on, things may repeat themselves, and the second time around will probably be more difficult.

Money

Your wallet will take a beating in June. You will be spending constantly and expect to spend the most during the second 10 days of the month. Overall, you are beginning a long period in which you will have to keep an eye on your money, as for various reasons, you may suddenly find yourself with much less of it.

Love and family

Your personal life is in a lull, right now. Your relationship with your spouse or better half might grow much cooler, or for various reasons, start to fade away.

In that case, the second 10 days of the month are the hardest. You may have a disagreement over various issues involving money, or alternatively, you may have clashing world views and values systems.

During the last 10 days of June, things will once again become peaceful, and you will be able to restore harmony to your lives. However, all year long, Jupiter is in the sector of the sky that is unfavorable to you, which means that your problems in June may repeat themselves from time to time.

Health

Those who manage to escape any professional or personal strife might instead face health issues.

Those who have old, chronic diseases might experience a relapse. The hardest time here is June 9-20, when, in addition to illnesses, you might also face a high chance of accidents and injury. It is not worth traveling during this time, either near or far, and the stars recommend being careful behind the wheel.

July

New York Time			London Time		
Calendar Day	Lunar Day	Lunar Day Start Time	Calendar Day	Lunar Day	Lunar Day Start Time
01/07/24	25	1.56 AM	01/07/24	25	1.30 AM
02/07/24	26	2.34 AM	02/07/24	26	1.58 AM
03/07/24	27	3.17 AM	03/07/24	27	2.32 AM
04/07/24	28	4.07 AM	04/07/24	28	3.16 AM
05/07/24	29	5.03 AM	05/07/24	29	4.10 AM
05/07/24	1	6.59 PM	05/07/24	1	11.59 PM
06/07/24	2	6.04 AM	06/07/24	2	5.13 AM
07/07/24	3	7.07 AM	07/07/24	3	6.21 AM
08/07/24	4	8.10 AM	08/07/24	4	7.32 AM
09/07/24	5	9.11 AM	09/07/24	5	8.42 AM
10/07/24	6	10.11 AM	10/07/24	6	9.50 AM
11/07/24	7	11.09 AM	11/07/24	7	10.57 AM
12/07/24	8	12.07 PM	12/07/24	8	12.03 PM
13/07/24	9	1.05 PM	13/07/24	9	1.09 PM
14/07/24	10	2.04 PM	14/07/24	10	2.16 PM
15/07/24	11	3.04 PM	15/07/24	11	3.24 PM
16/07/24	12	4.06 PM	16/07/24	12	4.34 PM
17/07/24	13	5.09 PM	17/07/24	13	5.43 PM
18/07/24	14	6.10 PM	18/07/24	14	6.48 PM
19/07/24	15	7.07 PM	19/07/24	15	7.46 PM
20/07/24	16	7.58 PM	20/07/24	16	8.35 PM
21/07/24	17	8.42 PM	21/07/24	17	9.13 PM
22/07/24	18	9.21 PM	22/07/24	18	9.44 PM
23/07/24	19	9.55 PM	23/07/24	19	10.09 PM
24/07/24	20	10.26 PM	24/07/24	20	10.31 PM
25/07/24	21	10.56 PM	25/07/24	21	10.52 PM
26/07/24	22	11.26 PM	26/07/24	22	11.12 PM
27/07/24	23	11.58 PM	27/07/24	23	11.35 PM
29/07/24	24	12.34 AM	29/07/24	24	12.01 AM
30/07/24	25	1.15 AM	30/07/24	25	12.33 AM
31/07/24	26	2.03 AM	31/07/24	26	1.14 AM

You can find the description of each lunar day in the chapter "A Guide to The Moon Cycle and Lunar Days"

This month is better than the last. You might not get everything you want on the first try, but be patient, and things will work out.

Work

The biggest trend this month is that you will be able to smooth over your relationship with colleagues in other cities or abroad. This will be thanks to your own efforts, as your business partners will not be trying too hard here. Many issues will be resolved in your favor now, but the problems will repeat themselves a little later.

Alternatively, you may have to grapple with legal issues from the past, but here, both old friends and new acquaintances will come to your aid. Keep in mind, however, that your legal issues are long and arduous, and highly unlikely to be resolved overnight. Each tiny step forward is vital through, and the road belongs to those who walk it.

Employees will also see improvements, though this process will take shape somewhat later. Another positive side of this month is that you will spend more time talking to old and new friends. You will need their support, both now and later on, so keep well-wishers around you, as it will make things much easier.

Money

Financially, the best time for you is during the second half of July. During this period, you will receive support from powerful Venus, which means that money will be coming in, and you can expect the largest sums on July 7, 8, 17, 19, 26, and 27.

Of course there are always expenses, but by the end of the month, you will still be in the black.

Love and family

Your personal life is also noticeably better these days. You are receiving support from Mercury, Venus, and the Sun, which will allow you to smooth over last month's disagreements, and you are sure to enjoy the sympathy of those around you.

Many Cancers will go on a trip and bring loved ones with them. The second half of the month is a good time to improve your home or successful shopping trips.

Those planning on buying a new home might make that happen during the last 10 days of the month.

Health

This month, you are feeling much better, but that's no reason to put yourself to the test with excess. You have the whole year ahead of you, and watching your health is going to be much more important than usual, especially if you are elderly or weakened. If that is you, lead a healthy lifestyle and regularly take preventive measures when it comes to chronic illnesses.

August

New York Time			London Time		
Calendar Day	Lunar Day	Lunar Day Start Time	Calendar Day	Lunar Day	Lunar Day Start Time
01/08/24	27	2.56 AM	01/08/24	27	2.03 AM
02/08/24	28	3.54 AM	02/08/24	28	3.02 AM
03/08/24	29	4.56 AM	03/08/24	29	4.08 AM
04/08/24	30	5.58 AM	04/08/24	30	5.17 AM
04/08/24	1	7.14 AM	04/08/24	1	12.14 PM
05/08/24	2	7.00 AM	05/08/24	2	6.27 AM
06/08/24	3	8.00 AM	06/08/24	3	7.36 AM
07/08/24	4	8.59 AM	07/08/24	4	8.43 AM
08/08/24	5	9.57 AM	08/08/24	5	9.50 AM
09/08/24	6	10.55 AM	09/08/24	6	10.55 AM
10/08/24	7	11.53 AM	10/08/24	7	12.02 PM
11/08/24	8	12.52 PM	11/08/24	8	1.09 PM
12/08/24	9	1.52 PM	12/08/24	9	2.17 PM
13/08/24	10	2.54 PM	13/08/24	10	3.25 PM
14/08/24	11	3.54 PM	14/08/24	11	4.31 PM
15/08/24	12	4.52 PM	15/08/24	12	5.32 PM
16/08/24	13	5.46 PM	16/08/24	13	6.24 PM
17/08/24	14	6.33 PM	17/08/24	14	7.07 PM
18/08/24	15	7.15 PM	18/08/24	15	7.42 PM
19/08/24	16	7.51 PM	19/08/24	16	8.10 PM
20/08/24	17	8.24 PM	20/08/24	17	8.33 PM
21/08/24	18	8.56 PM	21/08/24	18	8.55 PM
22/08/24	19	9.27 PM	22/08/24	19	9.17 PM
23/08/24	20	9.59 PM	23/08/24	20	9.39 PM
24/08/24	21	10.35 PM	24/08/24	21	10.05 PM
25/08/24	22	11.15 PM	25/08/24	22	10.35 PM
27/08/24	23	12.00 AM	26/08/24	23	11.13 PM
28/08/24	24	12.52 AM	28/08/24	24	12.00 AM
29/08/24	25	1.48 AM	29/08/24	25	12.56 AM
30/08/24	26	2.48 AM	30/08/24	26	1.59 AM
31/08/24	27	3.50 AM	31/08/24	27	3.07 AM

You can find the description of each lunar day in the chapter "A Guide to The Moon Cycle and Lunar Days"

Jupiter's, Mars's, and Saturn's aspects are in conflict, which may make August one of the most difficult months of the entire year. The stars recommend that you resolve any problems as they come, avoid rushing anything, and hold back if things don't go as you hoped and planned.

Work

This summer month, many Cancers who are part of the working world will face problems with roots in the past. You might see old legal issues rear their ugly heads again, which will open up some unpleasant circumstances for you. Alternatively, you will face unexpected complications involving colleagues in other cities or abroad, which will halt your cooperation for some time.

Employees would be wise to avoid any office gossip and rushing to take sides. Things might not be as they seem, so think hard before opening your mouth or making any moves.

Any Cancers would be wise to remember that this month will highlight your shortcomings, rather than your achievements. Your enemies and those who secretly wish you ill might take advantage of that. Expect intrigue, unnecessary conversations, and various disagreements to set the stage for this month. Be ready for all of August's turbulence and remember that after the storm, comes the sun.

Money

Your bank account leaves a lot to be desired this month. You won't end up penniless, but you will have a lot of expenses, which may be related to either business or your personal life.

Love and family

Cancers who are more focused on their personal life might face trouble, too. For various reasons, your relationship with relatives might grow more complicated. Perhaps you will disagree over money or become dissatisfied with an increasingly difficult relationship.

Couples will be disappointed in one another and face serious quarrels. Perhaps ill-wishers will meddle in your relationship to the point of you separating.

Be careful and watch your back. Remember that there will also be attempts at dragging your skeletons out of the closet.

Health

Those who are able to escape any work-related or personal strife unscathed might instead suffer health problems.

This month, you are feeling low, so there is a likelihood of old illnesses or unexpected new ones impacting your health.

August is also a month with a high chance of injuries. Be careful when traveling and driving and avoid any risky situations.

For everything, the second half of the month is the most dangerous time.

September

New York Time			London Time		
Calendar Day	Lunar Day	Lunar Day Start Time	Calendar Day	Lunar Day	Lunar Day Start Time
01/09/24	28	4.51 AM	01/09/24	28	4.16 AM
02/09/24	29	5.52 AM	02/09/24	29	5.25 AM
02/09/24	1	9.56 PM	03/09/24	1	2.56 AM
03/09/24	2	6.51 AM	03/09/24	2	6.32 AM
04/09/24	3	7.49 AM	04/09/24	3	7.39 AM
05/09/24	4	8.47 AM	05/09/24	4	8.45 AM
06/09/24	5	9.45 AM	06/09/24	5	9.51 AM
07/09/24	6	10.43 AM	07/09/24	6	10.57 AM
08/09/24	7	11.43 AM	08/09/24	7	12.04 PM
09/09/24	8	12.42 PM	09/09/24	8	1.11 PM
10/09/24	9	1.42 PM	10/09/24	9	2.17 PM
11/09/24	10	2.40 PM	11/09/24	10	3.19 PM
12/09/24	11	3.34 PM	12/09/24	11	4.14 PM
13/09/24	12	4.23 PM	13/09/24	12	5.00 PM
14/09/24	13	5.06 PM	14/09/24	13	5.37 PM
15/09/24	14	5.44 PM	15/09/24	14	6.07 PM
16/09/24	15	6.19 PM	16/09/24	15	6.33 PM
17/09/24	16	6.51 PM	17/09/24	16	6.56 PM
18/09/24	17	7.23 PM	18/09/24	17	7.18 PM
19/09/24	18	7.56 PM	19/09/24	18	7.40 PM
20/09/24	19	8.31 PM	20/09/24	19	8.05 PM
21/09/24	20	9.11 PM	21/09/24	20	8.35 PM
22/09/24	21	9.56 PM	22/09/24	21	9.11 PM
23/09/24	22	10.46 PM	23/09/24	22	9.55 PM
24/09/24	23	11.42 PM	24/09/24	23	10.49 PM
26/09/24	24	12.42 AM	25/09/24	24	11.51 PM
27/09/24	25	1.44 AM	27/09/24	25	12.58 AM
28/09/24	26	2.45 AM	28/09/24	26	2.07 AM
29/09/24	27	3.45 AM	29/09/24	27	3.16 AM
30/09/24	28	4.44 AM	30/09/24	28	4.23 AM

You can find the description of each lunar day in the chapter "A Guide to The Moon Cycle and Lunar Days"

Mars is in your sign for nearly all of September, which means that you will be bursting with energy. Your only responsibility is to use it for peaceful purposes.

Work

Cancers who are part of the working world will have to deal with yet another month of vigorously fighting back. You still have to deal with old legal issues, which may take a nasty turn, this time.

During the first 20 days of September, your foes may bring to light something you desperately wanted to keep quiet. That will have a major impact on the way things are going for you at work and tarnish your reputation.

Alternatively, you will face a very difficult relationship with colleagues in other cities or abroad, and in some cases, your cooperation will break down. Is that temporary or permanent? The astrologist predicts it will not last. In a few months, things will calm down and everything will fall back into place.

In September, you will do everything you can in order to resolve anything that comes your way, and you will have at least some success.

When things are looking difficult, lean on a friend for support, or someone highly placed in society. Their help is important, but the lion's share will fall on you.

Money

Financially, September is not great. Things look gloomy, and you may find yourself with absolutely no glimmers of light anywhere. However, things aren't all bad. In eight months, things will change for you. You just have to get through it right now, and there's no question you can do it.

Love and family

Cancers who are more focused on their personal life can expect problems that began in August to continue. You might not have resolved a disagreement with your relatives, or perhaps you will fight once again during the eclipse.

The darkest days are during the Full Moon from August 17-19, when the stars recommend that you be careful about what you do or say, in order to avoid any ruinous consequences. Mars in your sign might predispose you to conflicts, so remember that any peace is better than a good fight. Let that be your guide right now.

If you have any legal disputes involving family members, September is the best time to resolve them, as there is a high chance of losing in court is rather high.

Alternatively, a relative might fall ill or experience serious challenges, and will therefore need help in both words and deeds.

Health

In August, you have no reason to fear falling ill, but the stars urge you to be careful when driving or traveling.

The most difficult time is the first 20 days of the month, with the absolute worst on September 3, 4, and 16-19.

October

New York Time			London Time		
Calendar Day	Lunar Day	Lunar Day Start Time	Calendar Day	Lunar Day	Lunar Day Start Time
01/10/24	29	5.42 AM	01/10/24	29	5.30 AM
02/10/24	30	6.40 AM	02/10/24	30	6.35 AM
02/10/24	1	1.50 PM	02/10/24	1	7.50 PM
03/10/24	2	6.38 AM	03/10/24	2	7.41 AM
04/10/24	3	7.36 AM	04/10/24	3	8.48 AM
05/10/24	4	8.36 AM	05/10/24	4	9.55 AM
06/10/24	5	9.35 AM	06/10/24	5	11.02 AM
07/10/24	6	10.35 AM	07/10/24	6	12.08 PM
08/10/24	7	11.32 AM	08/10/24	7	1.11 PM
09/10/24	8	12.26 PM	09/10/24	8	2.07 PM
10/10/24	9	1.16 PM	10/10/24	9	2.55 PM
11/10/24	10	2.00 PM	11/10/24	10	3.34 PM
12/10/24	11	2.39 PM	12/10/24	11	4.06 PM
13/10/24	12	3.14 PM	13/10/24	12	4.33 PM
14/10/24	13	3.46 PM	14/10/24	13	4.56 PM
15/10/24	14	4.18 PM	15/10/24	14	5.18 PM
16/10/24	15	4.50 PM	16/10/24	15	5.40 PM
17/10/24	16	5.24 PM	17/10/24	16	6.03 PM
18/10/24	17	6.02 PM	18/10/24	17	6.31 PM
19/10/24	18	6.46 PM	19/10/24	18	7.04 PM
20/10/24	19	7.36 PM	20/10/24	19	7.46 PM
21/10/24	20	8.32 PM	21/10/24	20	8.38 PM
22/10/24	21	9.32 PM	22/10/24	21	9.39 PM
23/10/24	22	10.34 PM	23/10/24	22	10.47 PM
24/10/24	23	11.37 PM	24/10/24	23	11.56 PM
26/10/24	24	12.38 AM	26/10/24	24	1.06 AM
27/10/24	25	1.38 AM	27/10/24	25	1.14 AM
28/10/24	26	2.36 AM	28/10/24	26	2.20 AM
29/10/24	27	3.34 AM	29/10/24	27	3.26 AM
30/10/24	28	4.31 AM	30/10/24	28	4.32 AM
31/10/24	29	5.30 AM	31/10/24	29	5.38 AM

You can find the description of each lunar day in the chapter "A Guide to The Moon Cycle and Lunar Days"

You are embarking on a calm, steady month, which will allow you to take care of yourself and relax after all the stress you've been through lately. Rather than rushing to the barricades, strengthen your position!

Work

In October, business owners and managers will have to grapple with a disagreement involving business partners, and most likely, it will be over large property or real estate. Here, you might see some success, especially if you keep your ambition in check and make an effort to resolve things by reaching a compromise both sides can live with. Otherwise, you might be met with a fierce response.

Employees would be wise to steer clear of management. Any personal communication might end in a blowout, and remember, management always wins. If you really have to approach your superiors, it's best to do so in writing.

You might also take a few days off and spend time with yourself and your loved ones. The world won't stop turning if you are away from the office for a few days.

Money

Your financial situation is relatively stable and uninteresting, though you might receive a healthy profit from a successful real estate transaction. Some Cancers might also receive help from parents or an elderly family member.

Your expenses are low, and most of them are related to longstanding financial obligations, old debts, and your personal life.

Love and family

The major events of this month will probably be related to your personal life and family relationships. Spouses who get along will be immersed in improving their homes, and any arguments here might be a constant in the background all month long.

Your children will bring you joy, and you are likely to go on a trip together or visit your children who live in another city or abroad.

Things look quite different between separated or divorced couples. Here, you might have arguments of an entirely different nature over your home. You might struggle to divide your house, apartment, summer home, or other real estate. If you happen to have a shared business, things will only get worse.

Many Cancers will be acquiring new property, as foretold by the solar eclipse, which will accentuate the sector of the sky responsible for homes.

Health

This month, you are not feeling very energetic, but if you lead a healthy lifestyle and take care of yourself, any autumn colds will pass you by.

November

New York Time			London Time		
Calendar Day	Lunar Day	Lunar Day Start Time	Calendar Day	Lunar Day	Lunar Day Start Time
01/11/24	30	6.29 AM	01/11/24	30	6.45 AM
01/11/24	1	7.48 AM	01/11/24	1	12.48 PM
02/11/24	2	7.29 AM	02/11/24	2	7.53 AM
03/11/24	3	8.29 AM	03/11/24	3	9.00 AM
04/11/24	4	9.27 AM	04/11/24	4	10.04 AM
05/11/24	5	10.23 AM	05/11/24	5	11.03 AM
06/11/24	6	11.13 AM	06/11/24	6	11.53 AM
07/11/24	7	11.58 AM	07/11/24	7	12.34 PM
08/11/24	8	12.37 PM	08/11/24	8	1.08 PM
09/11/24	9	1.13 PM	09/11/24	9	1.35 PM
10/11/24	10	1.44 PM	10/11/24	10	1.58 PM
11/11/24	11	2.15 PM	11/11/24	11	2.20 PM
12/11/24	12	2.45 PM	12/11/24	12	2.40 PM
13/11/24	13	3.17 PM	13/11/24	13	3.02 PM
14/11/24	14	3.53 PM	14/11/24	14	3.27 PM
15/11/24	15	4.33 PM	15/11/24	15	3.57 PM
16/11/24	16	5.20 PM	16/11/24	16	4.35 PM
17/11/24	17	6.15 PM	17/11/24	17	5.22 PM
18/11/24	18	7.15 PM	18/11/24	18	6.21 PM
19/11/24	19	8.19 PM	19/11/24	19	7.28 PM
20/11/24	20	9.23 PM	20/11/24	20	8.39 PM
21/11/24	21	10.27 PM	21/11/24	21	9.51 PM
22/11/24	22	11.28 PM	22/11/24	22	11.01 PM
24/11/24	23	12.27 AM	24/11/24	23	12.09 AM
25/11/24	24	1.25 AM	25/11/24	24	1.15 AM
26/11/24	25	2.23 AM	26/11/24	25	2.21 AM
27/11/24	26	3.21 AM	27/11/24	26	3.27 AM
28/11/24	27	4.20 AM	28/11/24	27	4.33 AM
29/11/24	28	5.20 AM	29/11/24	28	5.41 AM
30/11/24	29	6.21 AM	30/11/24	29	6.49 AM

You can find the description of each lunar day in the chapter "A Guide to The Moon Cycle and Lunar Days"

In November, you would be wise to exercise caution. The path ahead is still long and winding, so remember that walking softly will take you a lot further.

Work

You are experiencing a somewhat difficult streak at work. Business owners and managers might find themselves audited, or legal trouble from the past may resurface, and your victory might be in doubt. If you can, put off any difficult decisions for a better time, that is, another six months, when the stars will be in a better position to help you.

You might experience minor friction within your team, which will get in the way of your productivity at work.

Employees' colleagues will gossip, and they may try to drag something you would rather keep quiet into the light.

The good news is that you will be busy developing your ties with colleagues in other cities or abroad. You will do everything you can in order to reconnect with old business partners living far away, and here, you can enjoy the tailwinds.

Money

Financially, November is full of challenges and turbulence. Your expenses are low, but your income is quite modest. You will be able to count on money coming in, however, on November 3, 4, 12, and 13, and the largest sum on 21-22.

Love and family

Your personal life looks sunnier, despite what is happening at work.

Parents will spend a lot of time with their children, which will bring them great joy. You might take a trip together, which will combine both business and pleasure, while also giving you new perspective on many situations. Even your expenses related to vacation and your children are not overwhelming, as you are able to take full advantage of everything.

Many couples will go on a trip together.

Rumors and gossip may cast a pall over November and set the stage for the entire month. Everyone has some skeletons in the closet, but you would be wise to make sure that yours stayed there, especially when it comes to people whose opinions you respect. This may begin in November and continue next month.

Health

This month, you may feel just like the capricious autumn weather.

You might feel amazing some days, while others, you may feel weak and fragile. You are able to stabilize this situation if you remember the importance of leading a healthy lifestyle and getting enough sleep.

December

New York Time			London Time		
Calendar Day	Lunar Day	Lunar Day Start Time	Calendar Day	Lunar Day	Lunar Day Start Time
1	01/12/24	1.22 AM	01/12/24	1	6.22 AM
2	01/12/24	7.21 AM	01/12/24	2	7.56 AM
3	02/12/24	8.18 AM	02/12/24	3	8.57 AM
4	03/12/24	9.11 AM	03/12/24	4	9.51 AM
5	04/12/24	9.58 AM	04/12/24	5	10.35 AM
6	05/12/24	10.39 AM	05/12/24	6	11.11 AM
7	06/12/24	11.15 AM	06/12/24	7	11.40 AM
8	07/12/24	11.47 AM	07/12/24	8	12.04 PM
9	08/12/24	12.17 PM	08/12/24	9	12.25 PM
10	09/12/24	12.46 PM	09/12/24	10	12.45 PM
11	10/12/24	1.16 PM	10/12/24	11	1.05 PM
12	11/12/24	1.48 PM	11/12/24	12	1.28 PM
13	12/12/24	2.25 PM	12/12/24	13	1.54 PM
14	13/12/24	3.07 PM	13/12/24	14	2.27 PM
15	14/12/24	3.58 PM	14/12/24	15	3.08 PM
16	15/12/24	4.55 PM	15/12/24	16	4.01 PM
17	16/12/24	5.58 PM	16/12/24	17	5.05 PM
18	17/12/24	7.04 PM	17/12/24	18	6.16 PM
19	18/12/24	8.10 PM	18/12/24	19	7.29 PM
20	19/12/24	9.13 PM	19/12/24	20	8.42 PM
21	20/12/24	10.15 PM	20/12/24	21	9.52 PM
22	21/12/24	11.14 PM	21/12/24	22	11.00 PM
23	23/12/24	12.12 AM	23/12/24	23	12.07 AM
24	24/12/24	1.10 AM	24/12/24	24	1.13 AM
25	25/12/24	2.09 AM	25/12/24	25	2.19 AM
26	26/12/24	3.08 AM	26/12/24	26	3.26 AM
27	27/12/24	4.08 AM	27/12/24	27	4.34 AM
28	28/12/24	5.09 AM	28/12/24	28	5.42 AM
29	29/12/24	6.08 AM	29/12/24	29	6.46 AM
30	30/12/24	7.04 AM	30/12/24	30	7.44 AM
1	30/12/24	5.27 PM	30/12/24	1	10.27 PM
2	31/12/24	7.54 AM	31/12/24	2	8.32 AM

You can find the description of each lunar day in the chapter "A Guide to The Moon Cycle and Lunar Days"

This month you would be wise to keep your ambitions in check, and generally be more modest. Your number one goal is to shore up your position and protect yourself, like any experienced warlord under siege.

Work

You are in for a turbulent month. Business owners and managers might run into audits, which will bring some skeletons in your closet to light.

This might involve old dealings which have unexpectedly taken on a new hue. Many Cancers will also have to grapple with old legal issues, and here, it is worth remembering that all of the failures you have faced in the past might repeat themselves once again. If things drag on, however, which is the most likely scenario, the best days ahead of you will start in April 2025.

What's more, managers are likely to have trouble involving subordinates, who might fail to carry out their responsibilities or clash with one another.

Employees can expect to disagree with colleagues or face intrigue and gossip or other breakdowns on their team.

Those planning any cooperation with colleagues in other cities or abroad will also face challenges this month. Business partners from afar might endure force majeure, which is becoming increasingly common in our world. You won't be bored in December, as you ward off attacks on all fronts.

Money

Financially, December is a difficult time for you, but things aren't entirely hopeless. You will have your normal income, and you can expect to receive the most money on December 1, 2, 10, 11, 18, 19, 28, and 29.

Love and family

Those who are primarily focused on their personal lives will have to deal with some tough times this month. You might see your relationship with relatives significantly worsen, and you may even have a serious argument or go your separate ways from a family member after a major misunderstanding.

Spouses will likely clash over money or how to raise their children. In December, it is a good idea to be attentive to one another, and if something goes wrong, you will have to simply accept it and get through it. This way, things will turn out better.

Those with real estate or other assets abroad will also be in for some turmoil.

In each specific case, it is impossible to predict what will happen, but there will definitely be cause for concern. Look at all potential options, and if you can, take steps ahead of time.

Any trips planned for December might be complicated or not turn out the way you had hoped and dreamed.

Health

Those who manage to get through December unscathed at work or at home might instead suffer in their health. You might see old illnesses resurface, or new ones unexpectedly appear. If that sounds like you, remember that carelessness toward yourself will turn out poorly this month, so if you run into any trouble, see a good doctor.

Be careful when traveling or driving.

Cancer Description

Sign. Feminine, water, cardinal.

Ruler. Moon.

Exaltation. Jupiter and Neptune in retrograde.

Temperament. Melancholic, with a tendency toward phlegmatic.

Positive traits. Adaptable, sensitive, romantic, intuitive, emotional, purposeful, patient, persistent, responsible, thrifty, caring, soft, restrained, imaginative, has a good memory.

Negative traits. Irritable, violently reactive, a tendency toward exaggeration, fearful, hysterical, cowardly, resentful, capricious, volatile, lazy, moody, passive, arrogant.

Weaknesses in the body. Stomach, digestive organs, pleura, mucous membranes, breasts, mammary glands, lymph.

Metal. Silver

Minerals. For a talisman – chrysoprase and emerald. In general: pearls, moonstone (selenite), opal.

Number. 5.

Day. Monday

Color. Bright green and purple.

Cancer energy

The volatile Moon changes phases four times in a month, making its children sensitive, easily influenced by their emotions, and mood swings. When Cancers are in a good mood, they are friendly and benevolent, but when their mood shifts to bad, it is best to avoid them. Cancers are forgiven for any mistake. What else would they do? After all, they are surprisingly cute and charming.

Despite the fact that Cancers are confident in themselves, they reach out to others. They have an undeniable talent for attracting others, because they need support and emotional energy from others. This is no surprise, given the fact that they are ruled by the Moon, which reflects the light of the Sun.

Cancer is a water sign, giving her an astuteness and intuition bordering on clairvoyance, as well as real skills at making money. Few others on the Zodiac are as adept at handling people and leveraging the energy of money. Cancers have turned this into an art form.

Astrological portrait of Cancer

Those born under Cancer are the most sensitive and emotional signs of the entire Zodiac. They have a rich spiritual life, which is always changing, just like the Moon, which is born, grows, climaxes, diminishes, and dies in order to do it all over again. Frequent mood swings are one of Cancer's traits. When Cancer is in a good mood, she is sweet, charming, and friendly. When she is in a bad mood, she has a tendency to slip into a long depression.

Cancer's motto is "I feel, therefore, I am". However, this does not mean we should assume that Cancer's heart is inherently warm or that she tends to feel sympathy for others. Cancers take much more than they give, and mainly have empathy for themselves. They will come to the rescue only when they can be convinced that there is no other option. Cancer seeks to be loved and cared for. However, she remains a bit of a mystery and will never fully reveal herself.

Cancers are vulnerable and sensitive to criticism and will react sharply to ridicule and sarcasm. Cancer is easily offended by a "wrong" look or tone. However, she is capable of defending herself. Cancer's self-defense mechanisms are very strong. A typical response is to lurk silently. Do not think for a second that she will forget or ignore what has happened, however. Cancer rarely forgives insults but believes that revenge is a dish best served cold. She might take a long time to come up with a plan for retaliation, and then leverage a convenient situation. It is best to stay neutral with a person like this.

Cancers tend to be successful people. They are not given to impulsivity or haste, but rather are cautious and risk-averse. Before doing anything, Cancer weighs the pros and cons. Only rarely will she listen to anyone else's advice. She prefers to resolve everything on her own and is not afraid of responsibility. Cancers do what they say and succeed at it. Mistakes are a rarity, thanks in large part to their outstanding intellectual abilities. Cancers perceive all nuances of what is happening around them. All of this is the influence of the Moon, which perceives and reflects the light of the Sun. Much like the Moon, Cancer perceives the outside world and immediately reflects it back.

Cancer's intuition is more developed than most other signs, meaning that she is excellent at understanding how other people are feeling and anticipating how situations will play out. Cancer is able to build a strong cause and effect relationship and find the root causes of certain problems, facts, and phenomena.

It is almost impossible to deceive a Cancer, and they should be treated with kindness. Pressuring them is useless – Cancer has developed a multi-stage defense mechanism, and the only way you can influence a Cancer is to pique her interest.

Cancers are persistent and assertive. If they have decided to do something, nothing will stop them. But in setting a goal, Cancer will never get straight to the point. Rather, she will bide her time, circle around the target, and keep an eye on it until she manages to reach it.

Despite Cancer's love of changes, novelty, and travel, they are strongly drawn to the home and their loved ones, especially their mother and children. To a Cancer, children are the world's greatest gift. Cancer is a home-bound and family sign, the keeper of family traditions. She adores her home and does not feel as relaxed and comfortable anywhere else.

If a Cancer is unable to achieve normal intellectual development, she might develop negative traits such as stinginess, childishness, or become conniving.

Cancers are often spilling over with emotions: it is normal for them to speak in loud tones, argue, or experience bouts of melancholy and even depression. This heightened sensitivity and vulnerability can eventually develop into complexes or neuroses. Cancer tries very hard to fulfill the ideal and be a strong person but continues to feel vulnerable.

Cancer is capable of seeing the true nature of the world around her and its essence, and carries higher ideas, and is a great zealot and creator. She passes all of the dirtiness in the world through her soul but holds onto her own pure soul. This is why it is wise to pay attention not only to a Cancer's outward appearance, but also her essence when dealing with her. If you manage to lure her out of her shell, you will be repaid in the highest form. After all, Cancer is not always on her best behavior, and not because she harbors any ill will. At her core, she is kind and selfless, due to her heightened sensitivity. Her soul cannot withstand the cruelty of the outside world. This might break Cancer, so she is forced to defend herself. If you cannot get her to open up, you will have to deal with her as though she were a child.

How to recognize Cancer by appearances

Cancer does not like to draw attention to herself, though she is very sociable by nature. She behaves modestly and exercises restraint. Cancers are rarely tall, and tend to be obese, though they often look more overweight than they really are, due to the roundness of their figure. They tend to have a round face, like the Moon, which may look childlike due to its puffiness. Their eyes are framed by long, thick eyelashes. They tend to gaze around themselves, often with a slightly sad look. Their thick eyebrows often meet over their nose, and their nose tends to be slightly upturned. Their lips are not distinctive, though often a bit smudged, puffy, and "sensual". Their hair is usually dark and curly, with pale skin and small hands.

Charting Cancer's Fate

Up until about 30-35 years of age, Cancer is fickle, full of worries, disappointments, and conflicts. They do not always succeed in marriage – divorce and separation are possible. Cancers are sensitive, vulnerable people, who depend on the opinions of others. They are characterized by volatile emotional outbursts. All of this may be a red flag to potential partners. This is why Cancers should be taught to reign in their temper from early childhood.

In adulthood, Fate rewards Cancers for all of the challenges they have faced. They will reach a decent position in society and earn a sizeable fortune.

It is important for Cancers to remember that in order to move forward, they need to always be looking backward, that is, to come back to their roots and build on the past. Roots are our first home and family. Build your own nest, and the rest will fall into place. Without a strong home, Cancers lack the support they need to succeed in society.

Excessive caution and suspiciousness can throw a wrench in Cancer's ability to succeed. Cancers are often prone to building safety nets where there is no threat.

A Guide to The Moon Cycle and Lunar Days

Since Ancient times, people have noticed that the moon has a strong influence on nature. Our Earth and everything living on it is a single living being, which is why the phases of the moon have such an effect on our health and mental state, and therefore, our lives. Remember Shakespeare and his description of Othello's jealousy in his famous tragedy:

"It is the very error of the moon, She comes more nearer Earth than she was wont And makes men mad."

If our inner rhythm is in harmony with that of the cosmos, we are able to achieve much more. People were aware of this a thousand years ago. The lunar calendar is ancient. We can find it among the ancient Sumerians (4000-3000 BC), the inhabitants of Mesopotamia, Native Americans, Hindus, and ancient Slavs. There is evidence that the Siberian Yakuts had a lunar calendar, as did the Malaysians.

Primitive tribes saw the moon as a source of fertility. Long before Christianity, the waxing moon was seen as favorable for planting new crops and starting a new business, for success and making money, while the waning moon was a sign that business would end.

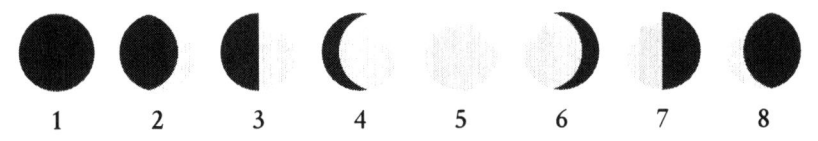

What are the phases of the moon?
- Phase 1 – new moon
- Phase 2 – waxing crescent moon
- Phase 3 – first quarter moon
- Phase 4 – waxing gibbous moon
- Phase 5 – full moon
- Phase 6 – waning gibbous moon
- Phase 7 – third quarter moon
- Phase 8 – waning crescent moon

To simplify things, we can divide the month into two phases:
- Waxing crescent moon - before the full moon
- Waning crescent moon - after the full moon

New Moon

We cannot see the new moon, as it is hidden. People might complain about feeling weak, mental imbalance, and fatigue. During this time, we want to avoid taking on too much or overdoing things. Generally, people are not very responsive and react poorly to requests, which is why it is best to look out for yourself, while not keeping your plate too full.

The new moon is a bad time for advertising – it will go unnoticed. It is not worth preparing any presentations, parties, or loud gatherings. People are feeling constrained, not very social, and sluggish.

This is also a less than ideal time for surgery, as your recovery will be slow, and the likelihood of medical error is high.

It is also difficult to get an accurate diagnosis during the new moon – diseases might seem to be hidden, and doctors might not see the real underlying cause of what ails you.

The new moon is also a bad time for dates, and sexual encounters may be dissatisfying and leave you feeling disappointed. Ancient astrologers did not advise planning a wedding night during the new moon.

Waxing crescent moon

It is easy to identify a waxing crescent moon. If you draw an imaginary line between the two "horns", you should see the letter P. The waxing moon is then divided into one and two quarters.

During the first quarter moon, we need to focus on planning – setting goals and thinking of how we will set about achieving them. However, it is still a good idea to hold back a bit and not overdo things. Energy levels are still low, though they are growing along with the moon. It is still a good idea to avoid any medical procedures during this time.

The second quarter is a time for bold, decisive action. Things will come easy, and there is a greater chance of a lucky break. This is a good time for weddings, especially if the moon will be in Libra, Cancer, or Taurus. Nevertheless, it is a good idea to put off any advertising activities and public speaking until closer to the full moon, if you can.

Full moon

During the full moon, the Earth is located between the sun and the moon. During this time, the moon is round and fully illuminated. This takes place during days 14-16 of the lunar cycle.

During the full moon, many people feel more vigorous than usual. They are emotional, sociable, and actively seeking more contact, so this may be a good time for any celebrations.

However, be careful not to drink too much – you can relax to the point that you lose control, and the consequences of that can be very unpleasant. If you are able to stick to moderation, there is no better time for a party!

The full moon is also the best time for advertising, as not only will your campaign be widely seen, people will be apt to remember it.

The full moon is also a favorable time for dates, and during this time, people are at their most open, romantic, and willing to tell each other something important that might take their relationship to the next level of trust and understanding.

Moreover, during the full moon, people feel a surge of energy, which may lead to hyperactivity, restlessness, and insomnia.

It will be harder to keep your emotions in check. You might face conflicts with friends, disasters, and accidents. During the full moon, any surgeries are **not a good idea**, as the risk of complications and bleeding is on the rise. Plastic surgery is also a bad idea, as swelling and bruises might be much worse than in another lunar phase. At the same time, the full moon is a good time to get an accurate diagnosis.

During this time, try to limit your calories and liquid intake (especially if you deal with bloating and excess weight), as your body is absorbing both calories and liquids faster during the full moon, and it can be very difficult to get rid of the weight later on.

Waning crescent moon

The full moon is over, and a new phase is beginning – the waning moon. This is a quieter time, when all of the jobs you started earlier are being partly or entirely completed (it all depends on the speed and scale).

Surgery will turn out much better if it is performed during the waning moon. Your recovery will be faster, and the likelihood of complications is much lower. If you have any plans to lose weight, the waning moon is the best time to do that. This is also a good time for quitting bad habits, such as smoking or cursing.

The waning moon can also be divided into the third and fourth quarters.

Third quarter - this is a favorable period, and you are able to resolve a lot of problems without conflict. People are calming down and ready to listen and take in information, while still being active. However, this is not the best time to begin any major projects, especially if you are unsure if you will be able to complete them by the start of the new lunar month.

The third quarter is a good time to get married, especially if the moon is in Cancer, Taurus, or Libra.

Fourth quarter – This is the most passive period of the lunar cycle. You are not as strong as usual. Your energy is lagging. You will be tired until reaching a new beginning. The best thing you can do as the lunar cycle comes to an end is to get things in order, and avoid anything that might get in your way at work or in personal relationships. Examine your successes and failures.

Now, let's discuss the lunar days in greater detail. For centuries, people around the world have described the influence of lunar days, and modern astrologers only add to this work, as they compare old texts to modern life.

The 1st lunar day

The first lunar day is extremely important for the rest of the lunar month. This is a much-needed day to carefully plan your activities and lay the groundwork for the rest of the lunar month. Remember that the first lunar day is not a good day for major activities, but rather for sitting down and planning things.

Avoid conflicts on this day, unless you want them to overshadow the rest of the month. Try to see the positive side of things and imagine that the lunar month will bring you good things both at work and in love. The more vividly you can imagine this, the sooner your desires will come to fruition. Perhaps it would be a good idea to jot down plans that will bring you closer to achieving your dreams. This is the best time for both manifesting and making wishes!

This is also a favorable day when it comes to seeking a new job or starting an academic program.

It is fine to go out on a date on the first lunar day, but limit any sexual contact, as your energy levels are low, and you are likely to end up disappointed.

Getting married on the first lunar day is not recommended.

Avoid getting a haircut – there are many indications that cutting your hair on the first lunar day will have a negative effect on your health and life expectancy.

Under no circumstances should you undergo any major cosmetic procedures, including plastic surgery. Energy levels are low, your skin is dull and almost stagnant. The results will not live up to your expectations, and in the worst-case scenario, you will end up looking worse than before. It is common for cosmetic procedures performed on this day to be disappointing or even useless. Even the best surgeons are less capable.

Your good dreams on the first lunar day foretell happiness and joy. Bad ones usually do not come true.

The 2nd lunar day

This is considered a lucky day, and is symbolized by a cornucopia. It is not an exaggeration to say that the second lunar day is a favorable time for both work and love. It is a time for action, and a great period to work on yourself, look for a new job, start something new, or complete any financial transaction, whether a sale or purchase. This is also a great time for creative and scientific insights, and a good time for any meeting – whether political or romantic.

Any romantic dates or sexual encounters during the second lunar day are unlikely to disappoint. This is also a good day for weddings or taking a trip with someone special.

During the second lunar day, the moon is beginning its waxing phase, which is a good time for anything you might to do nourish and restore your skin. This is a great time for any cosmetic procedures aimed at preservation, though it is best to put off any plastic surgery until the waning moon. If that is not possible, then the second lunar day is acceptable, if not ideal, and you will not run into any complications.

Folklore tells us that this is not a good day for a haircut, as that may lead to arguments with a loved one.

This is the best time for exercise – your body is in good shape, and you are able to handle new exercise regimens. If the moon happens to be in Scorpio, though, be careful.

This is a good day for anything positive, but avoid any conflicts, discussions about the status of your relationship, or litigation.

Dreams of the second lunar day are usually not prophetic.

The 3rd lunar day

On this day, we are usually able to make out a thin sliver of the lunar crescent. It is a longstanding tradition to show money during the new month – it is believed that as the moon grows, so will your savings.

However, astrological systems around the world consider this an unlucky, unfavorable day. It is not a good idea to travel, begin any new business, or give into your bad mood.

You might run into many a lot of problems at work on this day, which will cause you a lot of anxiety. However, it is a good day to take a step back and identify and set about fixing any flaws and shortcomings. Remember that everything tends to look worse on this day than it actually is.

It is not the time to ask management for anything – you are likely to walk away disappointed, and end up unfairly reprimanded rather than receiving a promotion or raise. Instead, focus on areas of work that need to be smoothed over or studied further. It will be clear what problems you are facing, and you will easily be able to find a remedy.

Do not rush to criticize your loved ones – things may not be as they appear. "Measure twice and cut once" is your motto on this day.

This is not a good day to get married, as the couple is likely to have a turbulent, short-lived marriage.

You can schedule a cosmetic procedure for this day, but only if it is relatively minor. Plastic surgery should wait.

Do exercises as usual, without overdoing it or adding any new routines.

Dreams on this day do not mean anything.

The 4th lunar day

These are relatively neutral days, in that they are unlikely to bring anything bad, but they also will not bring you any windfalls. The fourth lunar day is symbolized by a tree of paradise, the tree of knowledge, and the choice between good and evil. Things ultimately depend on us and our final decisions.

This is a great day for anything money-related – signing contracts, agreements, or even taking on credit. There are also a lot of contradictions on this day – on one hand, we are likely to receive money, which is a good thing, but on the other, we will have to give some of it away, which is never particularly fun or pleasant. There is good reason to consider all of your opportunities and possibilities before acting.

It is not a good day to get married, as the wedding will not be as fun as you had hoped. However, the fourth lunar day is, in fact, a good day for sex and conceiving a healthy child.

Be careful on this day if you happen to engage in any physical exercise, as it is not a good idea to overeat or abuse alcohol. Take care of yourself. Any illnesses which began on this day may be extremely dangerous, if they are not dealt with immediately.

Cosmetic procedures are not contraindicated, as long as they are to preserve your appearance. Plastic surgery can be performed if you truly feel it is necessary.

However, avoid getting a haircut, as it is unlikely to grow back healthily, and will become brittle and dull. However, if the moon is in Leo, you can disregard this advice.

Dreams may turn out to be real.

The 5th lunar day

Traditionally, the fifth lunar day is one of the worst of the lunar month. It is symbolized by a unicorn. Unicorns need to be tamed, but only a virgin is capable of doing so. Many people will feel drained on this day, or frustrated with themselves, those around them, and life in general.

Try to avoid arguments- any conflicts are likely to drag out for a long time, and then you may be overcome with guilt. This advice is relevant for both work and love.

Sexual encounters may be pleasant, but this is not a good day to plan a wedding, as it is likely to lead to a marriage full of unpleasant incidents.

Do not start any new businesses, or ask those around you for favors- you may be misunderstood and rejected.

It is fine to engage in physical exercise, but if you overdo it on this day, you may injure yourself.

Your energy levels are low. Cosmetic procedures may not be effective, and avoid any plastic surgeries.

It is good if you dream something connected with the road, trips or with movement in general. A bad dream might be a sign of a health problem which should be addressed.

The 6th lunar day

The symbol of the sixth lunar day is a cloud and a crane. This is a philosophical combination that suggests that it is not worth rushing things on these days. This is a very positive, lucky day for both work and love. Creative work will be especially successful, as will any attempts at opening a new business in your field.

The sixth lunar day is a good time for resolving any financial matters. There is one limitation, however – do not give anyone a loan, as they may not pay it back. But you can certainly sponsor and support those who are more vulnerable than you.

This day is a good time to go on a trip, whether close to home or far away.

This is also a good day for dates, weddings, and marriage proposals. Remember that energy is more romantic than sexual, so it is better to give the gift of roses and a bottle of champagne than hot, passionate sex.

It is a good idea to get some exercise, but do not overdo things, though you will probably not want to, either.

Cosmetic procedures will be successful, and you can even have plastic surgery performed, so long as the moon is not in Scorpio.

It is still a good idea to avoid getting your hair cut, as you might "cut off" something good in addition to your hair.

It is better to not discuss dreams as they are usually true. Your dreams of this day can remind you of something that needs to be completed as soon as possible.

The 7th lunar day

This is also a favorable lunar day, and it is symbolized by a fighting cock, which is an Avestan deity. Avoid any aggression on this day, and instead work on yourself, spend time at home or in nature. Avoid discussing the status of your relationship with anyone, arguing, or wishing bad things on anyone. Everything will come back to haunt you, remember, silence is golden.

Business negotiations and contracts will be successful. You can find support, sponsors, and people ready to help you in both words and deeds.

Lighten up with your colleagues and subordinates. Pay attention not only to their shortcomings, but also to their skills. This is a good day for reconciliation and creating both political and romantic unions.

The seventh lunar day is good for traveling, no matter how near or far from home.

It is also a favorable time for love and marriage.

Exercise moderately, and any plastic surgeries will go very smoothly, as long as the moon is not in Scorpio.

Dreams of this day may become a reality.

The 8th lunar day

The symbol for this day is a Phoenix, which symbolizes eternal rebirth and renewal, because this day is a great time for changes in all areas of your life. Your energy is likely to be high, and you want to do something new and unusual. This is a good time to look for a new job or begin studying something. Any out-of-the-box thinking is welcome, along with shaking things up a bit in order to improve your life.

However, avoid any financial transactions, as you may incur losses.

Avoid aggression. You can share your opinion by presenting well-founded arguments and facts, instead.

The phoenix rises from the ashes, so this is a good time to be careful with electrical appliances and fire in general. The risk of housefires is high.

Avoid any major financial transactions on the eighth day, as you may end up facing a series of complications. You can pay people their salaries, as this is unlikely to be a large sum.

This is a good day for weddings, but only if you and your future spouse are restless, creative souls and hope to achieve personal development through your marriage.

Any cosmetic procedures and plastic surgeries will go well today, as they are related to rebirth and renewal. Surgeons may find that they are true artists on this day!

You can try to change your hairstyle and get a fashionable haircut on this day.

You can trust your dreams seen on this day.

The 9th lunar day

The ninth lunar day is not particularly auspicious, and is even referred to as "Satan's" day. You may be overcome with doubt, suspicions, even depression and conflicts.

Your self-esteem will suffer, so don't overdo things physically, and avoid overeating or abusing alcohol.

This is a negative day for any business deals, travel, or financial transactions.

This is a particularly bad day for any events, so keep your head down at work and avoid any new initiatives.

It is better to avoid getting married on "Satan's" day, as the marriage will not last very long. Avoid sex, as well, but you can take care of your partner, listen them, and support them however they need.

Any cosmetic procedures will not have a lasting effect, and avoid any plastic surgery. A haircut will not turn out as you hoped.

Dreams of this day are usually prophetic.

The 10th lunar day

This is one of the luckiest days of the lunar month. It is symbolized by a spring, mushroom, or phallus. This is a time for starting a new business, learning new things, and creating.

The 10th lunar day is particularly lucky for business. Networking and financial transactions will be a success and bring hope. This is an ideal time for changing jobs, shifting your business tactics, and other renewals.

This is a perfect time for people in creative fields and those working in science, who may come up with incredible ideas that will bring many successful returns.

This is a very successful day for building a family and proposing marriage. This is a good time for celebrations and communication, so plan parties, meet with friends, and plan a romantic date.

One of the symbols for this day is a phallus, so sexual encounters are likely to be particularly satisfying.

The 10th lunar day is the best time to begin repairs, buying furniture, and items for home improvement.

You can exercise vigorously, and cosmetic procedures and plastic surgery will be very effective.

Dreams of this day will not come true.

The 11th lunar day

This is one of the best lunar days, and seen as the pinnacle of the lunar cycle. People are likely to be energetic, enthusiastic, and ready to move forward toward their goals.

The 11th lunar day is very successful for any financial transactions or business deals and meetings.

You might actively make yourself known, approach management to discuss a promotion, or look for a new job. This is an auspicious time for advertising campaigns, performances, and holding meetings.

Any trips planned will be a great success, whether near or far from home.

Romantic relationships are improving, sex is harmonious, and very desired.

Weddings held on this day will be fun, and the marriage will be a source of joy and happiness.

Exercise is a great idea, and you might even beat your own personal record.

This is an ideal time for any cosmetic procedures, but any more serious plastic surgeries might lead to a lot of bruising and swelling.

A haircut will turn out as you had hoped, and you can experiment a bit with your appearance.

You can ignore dreams of this day – usually they do not mean anything.

The 12th lunar day

This day is symbolized by the Grail and a heart. As we move closer to the full moon, our emotions are at their most open. During this time, if you ask someone for something, your request will be heeded. This is a day of faith, goodness, and divine revelations.

For business and financial transactions, this is not the most promising day. However, if you help others on this day, your good deeds are sure to come back to you.

This is a day for reconciliation, so do not try to explain your relationships, as no one is at fault, and it is better to focus on yourself, anyway.

Avoid weddings and sex on this day, but if you want to do what your partner asks, there is no better time.

Many may feel less than confident and cheerful during this day, so take it easy when working out. Avoid overeating, stay hydrated, and avoid alcohol.

The 12th lunar day is not the best for getting married or having sex, but the stars would welcome affection and a kind word.

Avoid getting a haircut, or any plastic surgeries. This is a neutral day for minor cosmetic procedures.

Nearly all dreams will come true.

The 13th lunar day

This day is symbolized by Samsara, the wheel of fate, which is very erratic and capable of moving in any direction. This is why the 13th lunar day is full of contradictions. In Indian traditions, this day is compared to a snake eating its own tail. This is a day for paying off old debts and returning to unfinished business.

Avoid beginning any new business on this day. It is preferable to finish old tasks and proofread your work. Information you receive on this day may not be reliable and must be verified.

It is worth resolving financial problems very carefully, and avoid arguments and conflict.

Do not change jobs on this day or go to a new place for the first time. Do not sit at home alone, though, go see old friends, parents, or older family members.

Minor cosmetic procedures are welcome on this day, but avoid any plastic surgery, as you may experience major swelling and bruising. Avoid any haircuts, too.

As a rule, all dreams will come true.

The 14th lunar day

It's a full moon! The 14th lunar day is one of the happiest, and it is symbolized by the trumpet. Pay attention – you may run into new, much-needed information. Networking will be successful, and you can confidently sign agreements, meet with people, and attend fun gatherings or other leisure activities. This is one of the best days for advertising, performances, and concerts, and those working in creative professions should keep this in mind, as should those who work in politics. Do not sit in place on this day – you need to get out and see others, make new connections, and try to be visible.

This is one of the best days for communication with and making requests from management, as your initiatives will be noticed and welcome. You might talk about a promotion, raise, or something similarly related to professional growth.

Couples will see their relationship is moving along well on this day, and it is also a good day for getting married.

Any sex on this day will be vigorous and memorable for a long time. The full moon is the best time for conceiving a child.

Any cosmetic procedures will be effective, but avoid any major changes to your appearance, as there is a high likelihood of bleeding and bruising. A haircut will turn out well.

Your dreams of this day will be more or less doubtful.

The 15th lunar day

It's a full moon! This day is symbolized by a serpent of fire. This is the energy peak of the entire lunar cycle, and a lot will depend on where you are focusing your energy.

You might face a lot of temptations on this day, for example, you might tell someone else's secret or your own to others, and come to regret it for a long time. The stars suggest exercising restraint in both your words and actions, as the 15th day of the lunar cycle is a day of deception and weaknesses.

This is a very active time, and many people might take unnecessary risks. This is not the best day for signing any agreements or contracts. For any performances, concerts, or advertising, however, this is one of the best days of the month.

You can get married on the 15th day, but only if you know each other well and have carefully considered your partnership, without any hasty decisions. This is also a favorable day for a second marriage.

Your romantic relationship is looking wonderful – you are on cloud 9, writing poetry, and deeply convinced of how right your partner is for you – and they feel the same way. It is important that this does not suddenly lead to an abrupt disappointment.

Avoid getting any haircuts on the 15th day of the month, as you may end up with a headache.

Conservative cosmetic procedures and creams will be very effective, but avoid any injections or plastic surgery today. Bleeding, swelling, and bruising are all but guaranteed.

Dreams on the 15th day nearly always come true.

The 16th lunar day

This day is symbolized by a dove. The full moon is over, and the moon is now in its waning phase. Usually, after the turbulent days of the full moon, people feel a bit under the weather. They are not cheerful, and want to avoid excess worry and give themselves a chance to breathe.

Don't ignore your body's wishes, take it easy with physical activities, and take some time for yourself. You might spend time in nature, in the forest, or at a country home.

The 16th day of the lunar month is a time for moderation in all areas – your behavior, eating, and even in your clothes. If you overate during the full moon period, now is the time to diet a bit or at least avoid fatty foods and meat.

This is not a promising day for resolving any financial matters. Keep your documents in order and get ready for any future meetings, instead. If you help a loved one, your good deed will come back 100 times over.

Avoid getting married today, as well as sex.

Cosmetic procedures are likely to be a success, especially if they are related to cleansing your skin, but it is best to avoid any plastic surgery or injections. Your body is not ready to accept them. A haircut will turn out as you hoped.

Any dreams are likely to come true, but that also depends on a correct interpretation.

The 17th lunar day

This day is represented by a vine and bell. It is a happy day and both successful and fun-filled. It is also a good time for negotiations, concluding small business deals, shaking up staffing, and creativity. However, you should keep in mind that the 17th day is only favorable for minor business, and you should avoid starting any major events.

Avoid any major financial transactions on this day. Do not give anyone money as a loan or borrow anything yourself, either.

Any travel, whether for business or pleasure, is likely to be a success.

The 17th day is a great time to get married, and an ideal day for dates. Any sexual encounters will bring you happiness and joy.

Avoid getting your hair cut on this day, but cosmetic procedures and plastic surgery will be a success. Women will look better than usual.

Your dreams are likely to come true in three days.

The 18th lunar day

This day is represented by a mirror. It is a difficult, and generally unpromising day, too. Just as the mirror reflects our imperfections back to us, we need to remember that moderation and modesty are key.

The 18th day is not a favorable time for any business meetings or financial transactions. You can, however work on jobs you already began. It is, however, a positive day for those who work in research or the creative fields.

Your motto of the day is to keep a cool head when it comes to your opportunities and the opportunities of those around you. This is relevant for both work and romantic relationships. It is not a good time to criticize others – any conflicts or arguments may lead to lasting consequences, which you do not need.

Avoid getting married on this day, as well as sexual encounters, which are likely to be disappointing. It is a good time to take a trip together, which will only be good for your relationship.

Avoid getting your hair cut, though this is a relatively neutral day for a haircut, which might turn out well, and though it will not exceed your expectations, it will also not leave you upset. Avoid any plastic surgeries.

Dreams on this day will come true.

The 19th lunar day

This is a very difficult day and it is represented by a spider. The energy is complicated, if not outright dangerous. Don't panic or get depressed, though – this is a test of your strength, and if you are able to hold onto all you have achieved. This is relevant for both work and love. On the 19th day, you should avoid taking any trips.

The energy of the 19th lunar day is very unfavorable for beginning any major projects, and business in general. Work on what you started earlier, get your affairs in order, think over your ideas and emotions, and check to make sure that everything you have done hitherto is living up to your expectations. Do not carry out any financial transactions or take out any loans – do not loan anyone else money, either. Do not ask your managers for anything as they are unlikely to listen to what you have to say, and make judgments instead.

This is a day when you might face outright deception, so do not take any risks and ignore rumors. Do not work on anything related to real estate or legal matters.

This is a very hard time for people with an unbalanced psyche, as they may experience sudden exacerbations or even suicidal ideations.

This is a very unlucky day to get married. Sexual encounters might be disappointing and significantly worsen your relationship.

Avoid any haircuts or cosmetic procedures or surgeries.

Your dreams of this day will come true.

The 20th lunar day

This is also a difficult day, though less so than the 19th. It is represented by an eagle. This is a good time to work on your own development and spiritual growth, by speaking to a psychologist or astrologer.

Avoid pride, anger, arrogance, and envy.

The 20th lunar day is a good time for people who are active and decisive. They will be able to easily overcome any obstacles, flying over them just like an eagle. If you have to overcome your own fears, you will be able to do so – don't limit yourself, and you will see that there is nothing to be afraid of. It is a good day for any financial transactions, signing contracts, and reaching agreements, as well as networking.

The 20th lunar day is a favorable time for those who work in the creative fields, as they will be able to dream up the idea that will open up a whole host of new possibilities. Avoid conflicts – they may ruin your relationship with a lot of people, and it will not be easy to come back from that.

This is a lucky day for getting married, but only if you have been with your partner for several years, now. Sexual encounters will not be particularly joyful, but they also will not cause you any problems.

Avoid getting your hair cut, but you can certainly get it styled. The 20th lunar day is a good day for those who are looking to lose weight. You will be able to do so quickly, and it will be easy for you to follow a diet.

Cosmetic procedures will be a success, as will any plastic surgeries.

Pay attention to dreams of this day as they are likely to come true.

The 21ˢᵗ lunar day

This is one of the most successful days of the lunar month, and it is symbolized by a herd of horses – imagine energy, strength, speed, and bravery. Everything you think up will happen quickly, and you will be able to easily overcome obstacles. A mare is not only brave but also an honest animal, so you will only experience this luck if you remember that honesty is always the best policy.

This is also a favorable day for business. Reaching new agreements and signing contracts, or dealing with foreign partners – it is all likely to be a success. Any financial issues will be resolved successfully.

Those in the creative world will be able to show off their talent and be recognized for their work. Anyone involved in the performing arts can expect success, luck, and recognition. A galloping herd of horses moves quickly, so you might transition to a new job, move to a new apartment, or go on a business trip or travel with your better half.

The 21ˢᵗ lunar day is one of the best to get married or have a sexual encounter.

This is a great time for athletes, hunters, and anyone who likes adventurous activities.

But for criminals and thieves, this is not a lucky or happy day – they will quickly be brought to justice.

Any haircuts or cosmetic procedures are likely to be a huge success and bring both beauty and happiness. You will recover quickly after any surgeries, perhaps without any swelling or bruising at all.

Dreams tend to not be reliable.

The 22ⁿᵈ lunar day

This day will be strange and contradictory. It is symbolized by the elephant Ganesha. According to Indian mythology, Ganesha is the patron saint of hidden knowledge. so this is a favorable day for anyone who is trying to learn more about the world and ready to find the truth, though this is often seen as a hopeless endeavor. This is a day for philosophers and wisemen and women. However, it is an inauspicious day for business, and unlikely to lead to resolving financial issues, signing contracts, agreements, or beginning new projects. You can expect trouble at work.

For creative people, and new employees, this is a successful day.

This is a good day for apologies and reconciliation.

Avoid getting married, though you can feel free to engage in sexual encounters.

For haircuts and cosmetic procedures, this is a fantastic day. Surgeries will also turn out, as long as the moon is not in Scorpio.

Dreams will come true.

The 23rd lunar day

This is a challenging day represented by a crocodile, which is a very aggressive animal. This is a day of strong energy, but it is also adventurous and tough. Your main task is to focus your energy in the right direction. There may be accidents, arguments, conflicts, fights, and violence, which is why it is important to strive for balance and calm.

Keep a close eye on your surroundings – there may be traitors or people who do not wish you well, so be careful.

However, this is still a favorable day for business – many problems will be resolved successfully. You are able to sign contracts and receive credit successfully, as long as you remain active and decisive in what you do.

This is not a day for changing jobs or working on real estate transactions or legal proceedings. This is not a favorable day for traveling, no matter how near or far you plan on going.

This is not a promising day to get married – things may end in conflict, if not an all-out brawl.

Sexual relations are not off the table, as long as the couple trusts one another.

Haircuts or cosmetic procedures will not turn out as you had hoped, so avoid them.

Dreams during this lunar day usually mean something opposite of what awaits you, so you can disregard them.

The 24th lunar day

This is a neutral, calm day that is symbolized by a bear. It is favorable for forgiveness and reconciliation.

This is also a good day for learning new things, reading, self-development, and taking time to relax in nature.

This is a great day for any type of financial activity, conferences, academic meetings, and faraway travel.

The 24th lunar day is a good time for love and getting married, as any marriage will be strong and lasting.

Cosmetic procedures and plastic surgery will be a success, and you can expect a speedy recovery.

Avoid getting a haircut on this day, however, as your hair will likely thin and grow back slowly.

Dreams of this lunar day are usually connected with your personal life.

The 25th lunar day

This is still another quiet day, symbolized by a turtle.

Just like a turtle, this is not a day to rush, and it is best to sit down and take stock of your life. This is a good time for resolving any personal problems, as the moon's energy makes it possible for you to calm down and find the right path.

This is also not a bad day for business. It is believed that any business you begin on this day is sure to be a success. This is especially the case for trade and any monetary activities.

The 25th lunar day is not a good day to get married, especially if the couple is very young.

This is a neutral day for sexual encounters, as the moon is waning, energy is low, so the decision is yours.

Avoid any cosmetic procedures, except those for cleansing your skin. This is not a favorable day for haircuts or plastic surgery – unless the moon is in Libra or Leo.

You can have a prophetic dream on this day.

The 26th lunar day

The 26th lunar day is full of contradictions and complicated. It is represented by a toad.

It is not time to start or take on something new, as nothing good will come of it. Avoid any major purchases, as you will later come to see that your money was wasted. The best thing you can do on this day is stay at home and watch a good movie or read a good book.

Avoid traveling on this day, as it may not turn out well.

The 26th lunar day is a negative day for any business negotiations and starting new businesses. Do not complete any business deals or financial transactions. Your colleagues may be arguing, and your managers may be dissatisfied. But if you have decided to leave your job, there is no better time to do so.

This is not a good day to get married, as both partners' expectations may fall flat, and they will soon be disappointed.

The waning moon carries a negative charge, so avoid any haircuts and surgeries, though you can get cosmetic procedures if they are relatively minor.

Your dreams will come true.

The 27th lunar day

The 27th lunar day is one of the best days of the month, and it is represented by a ship. You can boldly start any new business, which is sure to be promising. This is a great day for students, teachers, and learning new things. Any information that comes to you on this day may be extremely valuable and useful to you.

The 27th day is good for communication and travel, whether near or far from home, and no matter whether it is for work or pleasure.

This is also a good day for any professional activities or financial transactions. If there are people around you who need help, you must support them, as your good deeds will come back 100-fold.

Romantic dates will go well, though any weddings should be quiet and subdued. This is a particularly good day for older couples or second marriages.

The waning moon means that hair will grow back very slowly, but in general, you can expect a haircut to turn out well. This is a great day for plastic surgery or cosmetic procedures, as the results will be pleasing, and you will have a speedy recovery, without any bruising or swelling, most of the time.

However, beware if the moon is in Scorpio on this day – that is not a good omen for any plastic surgery.

Do not pay any attention to dreams on this day.

The 28th lunar day

This is another favorable day in the waning moon cycle, and it is represented by a lotus. This is a day of wisdom and spiritual awakening. If possible, spend part of the day in nature. It is important to take stock of the last month and decide what you need to do during its two remaining days.

This is a good time for any career development, changing jobs, conducting business, decision-making, and signing agreements, as well as going on a trip. You might conclude any business deal, hold negotiations, work with money and securities.

This is also a good day for any repairs or improvements around your home or apartment.

Any weddings today should be subdued and modest, and restricted to family members only. A loud, raucous wedding might not turn out very well.

Your hair will grow slowly, but any haircuts will turn out very elegant and stylish. Cosmetic procedures and surgeries are not contraindicated. You will recover quickly with little bruising and swelling.

Do not take any dreams too seriously.

The 29th lunar day

This is one of the most difficult days of the lunar month, and it is considered a Satanic day, unlucky for everyone and everything. It is symbolized by an octopus.

This is a dark day, and many will feel melancholy, depression, and a desire to simply be left alone. This is a day full of conflict and injuries, so be careful everywhere and with everyone. If you can, avoid any travel, and be particularly careful when handling any sharp objects. Do not engage in any business negotiations, sign any contracts, or take part in any networking.

Astrologers believe that anything you start on this day will completely fall apart. For once and for all, get rid of things that are impeding you from living your life. This is a good time to avoid people who you do find unpleasant.

This is also a time for fasting and limitations for everyone. Do not hold any celebrations, weddings, or have sexual relations – these events may not turn out as you hoped, and instead bring you nothing but suffering and strife.

Avoid getting a haircut, as well, as it will not make you look more beautiful and your hair will come back lifeless and dull. Cosmetic procedures can go ahead, but avoid any surgeries.

Dreams are likely to be true.

The 30th lunar day

There is not always a 30th lunar day, as some lunar months have only 29 days. This day is represented by a swan. The 30th lunar day is usually very short, and sometimes, it lasts less than an hour. This is a time for forgiveness and calm.

You might take stock of the last month, while also avoiding anything you do not need around you. Pay back loans, make donations, reconcile with those who recently offended you, and stop speaking to people who cause you suffering.

This is a good time for tying up loose ends, and many astrologers believe that it is also a good day to start new business.

However, avoid celebrations or weddings on this day. Spouses will either not live long, or they will quickly grow apart.

Do not get a haircut on this day, though cosmetic procedures are possible, as long as you avoid any surgeries.

Dreams promise happiness and should come true.

A Guide to Zodiac Compatibility

Often, when we meet a person, we get a feeling that they are good and we take an instant liking to them. Another person, however, gives us immediate feelings of distrust, fear and hostility. Is there an astrological reason why people say that 'the first impression is the most accurate'? How can we detect those who will bring us nothing but trouble and unhappiness?

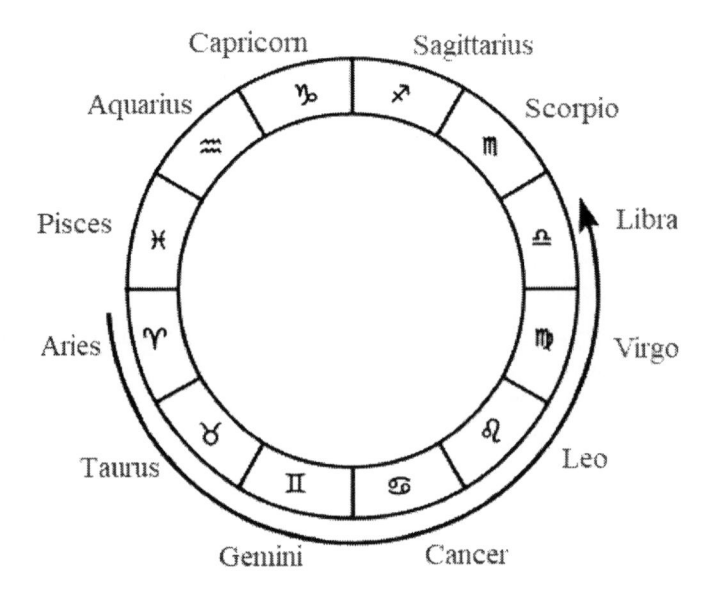

Without going too deeply into astrological subtleties unfamiliar to some readers, it is possible to determine the traits according to which friendship, love or business relationships will develop.

Let's begin with problematic relationships - our most difficult are with our **8th sign**. For example, for Aries the 8th sign is Scorpio, for Taurus it is Sagittarius and so on. Finding your 8th sign is easy; assume your own sign to be first (see above Figure) and then move eight signs counter clockwise around the Zodiac circle. This is also how the other signs (fourth, ninth and so on) that we mention are to be found.

Ancient astrologers variously referred to the 8th sign as the symbol of death, of destruction, of fated love or unfathomable attraction. In astrological terms, this pair is called 'master and slave' or 'boa constrictor and rabbit', with the role of 'master' or 'boa constrictor' being played by our 8th sign.

This relationship is especially difficult for politicians and business people.

We can take the example of a recent political confrontation in the USA. Hilary Clinton is a Scorpio while Donald Trump is a Gemini - her 8th sign. Even though many were certain that Clinton would be elected President, she lost.

To take another example, Hitler was a Taurus and his opponents – Stalin and Churchill - were both of his 8th sign, Sagittarius. The result of their confrontation is well known. Interestingly, the Russian Marshals who dealt crushing military blows to Hitler and so helped end the Third Reich - Konstantin Rokossovsky and Georgy Zhukov - were also Sagittarian, Hitler's 8th sign.

In another historical illustration, Lenin was also a Taurus. Stalin was of Lenin's 8th sign and was ultimately responsible for the downfall and possibly death of his one-time comrade-in-arms.

Business ties with those of our 8th sign are hazardous as they ultimately lead to stress and loss; both financial and moral. So, do not tangle with your 8th sign and never fight with it - your chances of winning are remote!

Such relationships are very interesting in terms of love and romance, however. We are magnetically attracted to our 8th sign and even though it may be very intense physically, it is very difficult for family life;

'Feeling bad when together, feeling worse when apart'.

As an example, let us take the famous lovers - George Sand who was Cancer and Alfred de Musset who was Sagittarius. Cancer is the 8th sign for Sagittarius, and the story of their crazy two-year love affair was the subject of much attention throughout France. Critics and writers were divided into 'Mussulist' and 'Sandist' camps; they debated fiercely about who was to blame for the sad ending to their love story - him or her. It's hard to imagine the energy needed to captivate the public for so long, but that energy was destructive for the couple. Passion raged in their hearts, but neither of them was able to comprehend their situation.

Georges Sand wrote to Musset, *"I don't love you anymore, and I will always adore you. I don't want you anymore, and I can't do without you. It seems that nothing but a heavenly lightning strike can heal me by destroying me. Good-bye! Stay or go, but don't say that I am not suffering. This is the only thing that can make me suffer even more, my love, my life, my blood! Go away, but kill me, leaving."* Musset replied only in brief, but its power surpassed Sand's tirade, *"When you embraced me, I felt something that is still bothering me, making it impossible for me to approach another woman."* These two people loved each other passionately and for two years lived together in a powder keg of passion, hatred and treachery.

When someone enters into a romantic liaison with their 8th sign, there will be no peace; indeed, these relationships are very attractive to those who enjoy the edgy, the borderline and, in the Dostoevsky style, the melodramatic. The first to lose interest in the relationship is, as a rule, the 8th sign.

If, by turn of fate, our child is born under our 8th sign, they will be very different from us and, in some ways, not live up to our expectations. It may be best to let them choose their own path.

In business and political relationships, the combination with our **12th sign** is also a complicated one.

We can take two political examples. Angela Merkel is a Cancer while Donald Trump is a Gemini - her 12th sign. This is why their relations are strained and complicated and we can even perhaps assume that the American president will achieve his political goals at her expense. Boris Yeltsin (Aquarius) was the 12th sign to Mikhail Gorbachev (Pisces) and it was Yeltsin who managed to dethrone the champion of Perestroika.

Even ancient astrologers noticed that our relationships with our 12th signs can never develop evenly; it is one of the most curious and problematic combinations. They are our hidden enemies and they seem to be digging a hole for us; they ingratiate themselves with us, discover our innermost secrets. As a result, we become bewildered and make mistakes when we deal with them. Among the Roman emperors murdered by members of their entourage, there was an interesting pattern - all the murderers were the 12th sign of the murdered.

We can also see this pernicious effect in Russian history: the German princess Alexandra (Gemini) married the last Russian Tsar Nicholas II (Taurus) - he was her 12th sign and brought her a tragic death. The wicked genius Grigory Rasputin (Cancer) made friends with Tsarina Alexandra, who was his 12th sign, and was murdered as a result of their odd friendship. The weakness of Nicholas II was exposed, and his authority reduced after the death of the economic and social reformer Pyotr Stolypin, who was his 12th sign. Thus, we see a chain of people whose downfall was brought about by their 12th sign.

So, it makes sense to be cautious of your 12th sign, especially if you have business ties. Usually, these people know much more about us than we want them to and they will often reveal our secrets for personal gain if it suits them. However, the outset of these relationships is, as a rule, quite normal - sometimes the two people will be friends, but sooner or later one will betray the other one or divulge a secret; inadvertently or not.

In terms of romantic relationships, our 12th sign is gentle, they take care of us and are tender towards us. They know our weaknesses well but accept them with understanding. It is they who guide us, although sometimes almost imperceptibly. Sexual attraction is usually strong.

For example, Meghan Markle is a Leo, the 12th sign for Prince Harry, who is a Virgo. Despite Queen Elizabeth II being lukewarm about the match, Harry's love was so strong that they did marry.

If a child is our 12th sign, it later becomes clear that they know all our secrets, even those that they are not supposed to know. It is very difficult to control them as they do everything in their own way.

Relations with our **7th sign** are also interesting. They are like our opposite; they have something to learn from us while we, in turn, have something to learn from them. This combination, in business and personal relationships, can be very positive and stimulating provided that both partners are quite intelligent and have high moral standards but if not, constant misunderstandings and challenges follow. Marriage or co-operation with the 7th sign can only exist as the union of two fully-fledged individuals and in this case love, significant business achievements and social success are possible.

However, the combination can be not only interesting, but also quite complicated.

An example is Angelina Jolie, a Gemini, and Brad Pitt, a Sagittarius. This is a typical bond with a 7th sign - it's lively and interesting, but rather stressful. Although such a couple may quarrel and even part from time to time, never do they lose interest in each other.

This may be why this combination is more stable in middle-age when there is an understanding of the true nature of marriage and partnership. In global, political terms, this suggests a state of eternal tension - a cold war - for example between Yeltsin (Aquarius) and Bill Clinton (Leo).

Relations with our **9th sign** are very good; they are our teacher and advisor - one who reveals things we are unaware of and our relationships with them very often involve travel or re-location. The combination can lead to spiritual growth and can be beneficial in terms of business.

Although, for example, Trump and Putin are political opponents, they can come to an understanding and even feel a certain sympathy for each other because Putin is a Libra while Trump is a Gemini, his 9th sign.

This union is also quite harmonious for conjugal and romantic relationships.

We treat our **3rd sign** somewhat condescendingly. They are like our younger siblings; we teach them and expect them to listen attentively. Our younger brothers and sisters are more often than not born under this sign. In terms of personal and sexual relationships, the union is not very inspiring and can end quickly, although this is not always the case. In terms of business, it is fairly average as it often connects partners from different cities or countries.

We treat our **5th sign** as a child and we must take care of them accordingly. The combination is not very good for business, however, since our 5th sign triumphs over us in terms of connections and finances, and thereby gives us very little in return save for love or sympathy. However, they are very good for family and romantic relationships, especially if the 5th sign is female. If a child is born as a 5th sign to their parents, their relationship will be a mutually smooth, loving and understanding one that lasts a lifetime.

Our **10th sign** is a born leader. Depending on the spiritual level of those involved, both pleasant and tense relations are possible; the relationship is often mutually beneficial in the good times but mutually disruptive in the bad times. In family relations, our 10th sign always tries to lead and will do so according to their intelligence and upbringing.

Our **4th sign** protects our home and can act as a sponsor to strengthen our financial or moral positions. Their advice should be heeded in all cases as it can be very effective, albeit very unobtrusive. If a woman takes this role, the relationship can be long and romantic, since all the spouse's wishes are usually met one way or another. Sometimes, such couples achieve great social success; for instance, Hilary Clinton, a Scorpio is the 4th sign to Bill Clinton, a Leo. On the other hand, if the husband is the 4th sign for his wife, he tends to be henpecked. There is often a strong sexual attraction. Our 4th sign can improve our living conditions and care for us in a parental way. If a child is our 4th sign, they are close to us and support us affectionately.

Relations with our **11th sign** are often either friendly or patronizing; we treat them reverently, while they treat us with friendly condescension. Sometimes, these relationships develop in an 'older brother' or 'high-ranking friend' sense; indeed, older brothers and sisters are often our 11th sign. In terms of personal and sexual relationships, our 11th sign is always inclined to enslave us. This tendency is most clearly manifested in such alliances as Capricorn and Pisces or Leo and Libra. A child who is the 11th sign to their parents will achieve greater success than their parents, but this will only make the parents proud.

Our **2nd sign** should bring us financial or other benefits; we receive a lot from them in both our business and our family life. In married couples, the 2nd sign usually looks after the financial situation for the benefit of the family. Sexual attraction is strong.

Our **6th sign** is our 'slave'; we always benefit from working with them and it's very difficult for them to escape our influence. In the event of hostility, especially if they have provoked the conflict, they receive a powerful retaliatory strike. In personal relations, we can almost destroy them by making them dance to our tune. For example, if a husband doesn't allow his wife to work or there are other adverse family circumstances, she gradually becomes lost as an individual despite being surrounded by care. This is the best-case scenario; worse outcomes are possible. Our 6th sign has a strong sexual attraction to us because we are the fatal 8th sign for them; we cool down quickly, however, and often make all kinds of demands. If the relationship with our 6th sign is a long one, there is a danger that routine, boredom and stagnation will ultimately destroy the relationship. A child born under our 6th sign needs particularly careful handling as they can feel fear or embarrassment when communicating with us. Their health often needs increased attention and we should also remember that they are very different from us emotionally.

Finally, we turn to relations with **our own sign**. Scorpio with Scorpio and Cancer with Cancer get along well, but in most other cases, however, our own sign is of little interest to us as it has a similar energy. Sometimes, this relationship can develop as a rivalry, either in business or in love.

There is another interesting detail - we are often attracted to one particular sign. For example, a man's wife and mistress often have the same sign. If there is confrontation between the two, the stronger character displaces the weaker one. As an example, Prince Charles is a Scorpio, while both Princess Diana and Camilla Parker Bowles were born under the sign of Cancer. Camilla was the more assertive and became dominant.

Of course, in order to draw any definitive conclusions, we need an individually prepared horoscope, but the above always, one way or another, manifests itself.

Love Description of Zodiac Signs

We know that human sexual behavior has been studied at length. Entire libraries have been written about it, with the aim of helping us understand ourselves and our partners. But is that even possible? It may not be; no matter how smart we are, when it comes to love and sex, there is always an infinite amount to learn. But we have to strive for perfection, and astrology, with its millennia of research, twelve astrological types, and twelve zodiac signs, may hold the key. Below, you will find a brief and accurate description of each zodiac sign's characteristics in love, for both men and women.

Men

ARIES

Aries men are not particularly deep or wise, but they make up for it in sincerity and loyalty. They are active, even aggressive lovers, but a hopeless romantic may be lurking just below the surface. Aries are often monogamous and chivalrous men, for whom there is only one woman (of course, in her absence, they can sleep around with no remorse). If the object of your affection is an Aries, be sure to give him a lot of sex, and remember that for an Aries, when it comes to sex, anything goes. Aries cannot stand women who are negative or disheveled. They need someone energetic, lively, and to feel exciting feelings of romance.

The best partner for an Aries is Cancer, Sagittarius, or Leo. Aquarius can also be a good match, but the relationship will be rather friendly in nature. Partnering with a Scorpio or Taurus will be difficult, but they can be stimulating lovers for an Aries. Virgos are good business contacts, but a poor match as lovers or spouses.

TAURUS

A typical Taurean man is warm, friendly, gentle, and passionate, even if he doesn't always show it. He is utterly captivated by the beauty of the female body, and can find inspiration in any woman. A Taurus has such excess physical and sexual prowess, that to him, sex is a way to relax and calm down. He is the most passionate and emotional lover of the Zodiac, but he expects his partner to take the initiative, and if she doesn't, he will easily find someone else. Taureans rarely divorce, and are true to the end – if not sexually, at least spiritually. They are secretive, keep their cards close, and may have secret lovers. If a Taurus does not feel a deep emotional connection with someone, he won't be shy to ask her friends for their number. He prefers a voluptuous figure over an athletic or skinny woman.

The best partners for a Taurus are Cancer, Virgo, Pisces, or Scorpio. Sagittarius can show a Taurus real delights in both body and spirit, but they are unlikely to make it down the aisle. They can have an interesting relationship with an Aquarius – these signs are very different, but sometimes can spend their lives together. They might initially feel attracted to an Aries, before rejecting her.

GEMINI

The typical Gemini man is easygoing and polite. He is calm, collected, and analytical. For a Gemini, passion is closely linked to intellect, to the point that they will try to find an explanation for their actions before carrying them out. But passion cannot be explained, which scares a Gemini, and they begin jumping from one extreme to the other. This is why you will find more bigamists among Geminis than any other sign of the Zodiac. Sometimes, Gemini men even have two families, or divorce and marry several times throughout the course of their lives. This may be because they simply can't let new and interesting experiences pass them by. A Gemini's wife or lover needs to be smart, quick, and always looking ahead. If she isn't, he will find a new object for his affection.

Aquarians, Libras, and Aries make good partners for a Gemini. A Sagittarius can be fascinating for him, but they will not marry before he reaches middle age, as both partners will be fickle while they are younger. A Gemini and Scorpio are likely to be a difficult match, and the Gemini will try to wriggle out of the Scorpio's tight embrace. A Taurus will be an exciting sex partner, but their partnership won't be for long, and the Taurus is often at fault.

CANCER

Cancers tend to be deep, emotional individuals, who are both sensitive and highly sexual. Their charm is almost mystical, and they know how to use it. Cancers may be the most promiscuous sign of the Zodiac, and open to absolutely anything in bed. Younger Cancers look for women who are more mature, as they are skilled lovers. As they age, they look for someone young enough to be their own daughter, and delight in taking on the role of a teacher. Cancers are devoted to building a family and an inviting home, but once they achieve that goal, they are likely to have a wandering eye. They will not seek moral justification, as they sincerely believe it is simply something everyone does. Their charm works in such a way that women are deeply convinced they are the most important love in a Cancer's life, and that circumstances are the only thing preventing them from being together. Remember that a Cancer man is a master manipulator, and will not be yours unless he is sure you have throngs of admirers. He loves feminine curves, and is turned on by exquisite fragrances. Cancers don't end things with old lovers, and often go back for a visit after a breakup. Another type of Cancer is rarer – a faithful friend, and up for anything in order to provide for his wife and children. He is patriotic and a responsible worker.

Scorpios, Pisces, and other Cancers are a good match. A Taurus can make for a lasting relationship, as both signs place great value on family and are able to get along with one another. A Sagittarius will result in fights and blowouts from the very beginning, followed by conflicts and breakups. The Sagittarius will suffer the most. Marriage to an Aries isn't off the table, but it won't last very long.

LEO

A typical Leo is handsome, proud, and vain, with a need to be the center of attention at all times. They often pretend to be virtuous, until they are able to actually master it. They crave flattery, and prefer women who comply and cater to them. Leos demand unconditional obedience, and constant approval. When a Leo is in love, he is fairly sexual, and capable of being devoted and faithful. Cheap love affairs are not his thing, and Leos are highly aware of how expensive it is to divorce. They make excellent fathers. A Leo's partner needs to look polished and well-dressed, and he will not tolerate either frumpiness or nerds.

Aries, Sagittarius, and Gemini make for good matches. Leos are often very beguiling to Libras; this is the most infamous astrological "master-slave" pairing. Leos are also inexplicably drawn to Pisces – this is the only sign capable of taming them. A Leo and Virgo will face a host of problems sooner or later, and they might be material in nature. The Virgo will attempt to conquer him, and if she does, a breakup is inevitable.

VIRGO

Virgo is a highly intellectual sign, who likes to take a step back and spend his time studying the big picture. But love inherently does not lend itself to analysis, and this can leave Virgos feeling perplexed. While Virgo is taking his time, studying the object of his affection, someone else will swoop in and take her away, leaving him bitterly disappointed. Perhaps for that reason, Virgos tend to marry late, but once they are married, they remain true, and hardly ever initiate divorce. In bed, they are modest and reserved, as they see sex as some sort of quirk of nature, designed solely for procreation. Most Virgos have a gifted sense of taste, hearing, and smell. They cannot tolerate pungent odors and can be squeamish; they believe their partners should always take pains to be very clean. Virgos usually hate over-the-top expressions of love, and are immune to sex as a mean s of control. Many Virgos are stingy and more appropriate as husbands than lovers. Male Virgos tend to be monogamous, though if they are unhappy or disappointed with their partner, they may begin to look for comfort elsewhere and often give in to drunkenness.

Taurus, Capricorn, and Scorpio make the best partners for a Virgo. They may feel inexplicable attraction for Aquarians. They will form friendships with Aries, but rarely will this couple make it down the aisle. With Leos, be careful – this sign is best as a lover, not a spouse.

LIBRA

Libra is a very complex, wishy-washy sign. They are constantly seeking perfection, which often leaves them in discord with the reality around them. Libra men are elegant and refined, and expect no less from their partner. Many Libras treat their partners like a beautiful work of art, and have trouble holding onto the object of their affection. They view love itself as a very abstract concept, and can get tired of the physical aspect of their relationship. They are much more drawn to intrigue and the chase- dreams, candlelit evenings, and other symbols of romance. A high percentage of Libra men are gay, and they view sex with other men as the more elite option. Even when Libras are unhappy in their marriages, they never divorce willingly. Their wives might leave them, however, or they might be taken away by a more decisive partner.

Aquarius and Gemini make the best matches for Libras. Libra can also easily control an independent Sagittarius, and can easily fall under the influence of a powerful and determined Leo, before putting all his strength and effort into breaking free. Relationships with Scorpios are difficult; they may become lovers, but will rarely marry.

SCORPIO

Though it is common to perceive Scorpios as incredibly sexual, they are, in fact, very unassuming, and never brag about their exploits. They will, however, be faithful and devoted to the right woman. The Scorpio man is taciturn, and you can't expect any tender words from him, but he will defend those he loves to the very end. Despite his outward control, Scorpio is very emotional; he needs and craves love, and is willing to fight for it. Scorpios are incredible lovers, and rather than leaving them tired, sex leaves them feeling energized. They are always sexy, even if they aren't particularly handsome. They are unconcerned with the ceremony of wooing you, and more focused on the act of love itself.

Expressive Cancers and gentle, amenable Pisces make the best partners. A Scorpio might also fall under the spell of a Virgo, who is adept at taking the lead. Sparks might fly between two Scorpios, or with a Taurus, who is perfect for a Scorpio in bed. Relationships with Libras, Sagittarians, and Aries are difficult.

SAGITTARIUS

Sagittarian men are lucky, curious, and gregarious. Younger Sagittarians are romantic, passionate, and burning with desire to experience every type of love. Sagittarius is a very idealistic sign, and in that search for perfection, they tend to flit from one partner to another, eventually forgetting what they were even looking for in the first place. A negative Sagittarius might have two or three relationships going on at once, assigning each partner a different day of the week. On the other hand, a positive Sagittarius will channel his powerful sexual energy into creativity, and take his career to new heights. Generally speaking, after multiple relationships and divorces, the Sagittarian man will conclude that his ideal marriage is one where his partner is willing to look the other way.

Aries and Leo make the best matches for a Sagittarius. He might fall under the spell of a Cancer, but would not be happy being married to her. Gemini can be very intriguing, but will only make for a happy marriage after middle age, when both partners are older and wiser. Younger Sagittarians often marry Aquarian women, but things quickly fall apart. Scorpios can make for an interesting relationship, but if the Sagittarius fails to comply, divorce is inevitable.

CAPRICORN

Practical, reserved Capricorn is one of the least sexual signs of the Zodiac. He views sex as an idle way to pass the time, and something he can live without, until he wants to start a family. He tends to marry late, and almost never divorces. Young Capricorns are prone to suppressing their sexual desires, and only discover them later in life, when they have already achieved everything a real man needs – a career and money. We'll be frank – Capricorn is not the best lover, but he can compensate by being caring, attentive, and showering you with valuable gifts. Ever cautious, Capricorn loves to schedule his sexual relationships, and this is something partners will just have to accept. Women should understand that Capricorn needs some help relaxing – perhaps with alcohol. They prefer inconspicuous, unassuming women, and run away from a fashion plate.

The best partners for a Capricorn are Virgo, Taurus, or Scorpio. Cancers might catch his attention, and if they marry, it is likely to be for life. Capricorn is able to easily dominate Pisces, and Pisces-Capricorn is a well-known "slave and master" combination. Relationships with Leos tend to be erratic, and they are unlikely to wed. Aries might make for a cozy family at first, but things will cool off quickly, and often, the marriage only lasts as long as Capricorn is unwilling to make a change in his life.

AQUARIUS

Aquarian men are mercurial, and often come off as peculiar, unusual, or aloof, and detached. Aquarians are turned on by anything novel or strange, and they are constantly looking for new and interesting people. They are stimulated by having a variety of sexual partners, but they consider this to simply be normal life, rather than sexually immoral. Aquarians are unique – they are more abstract than realistic, and can be cold and incomprehensible, even in close relationships. Once an Aquarius gets married, he will try to remain within the realm of decency, but often fails. An Aquarian's partners need uncommon patience, as nothing they do can restrain him. Occasionally, one might encounter another kind of Aquarius – a responsible, hard worker, and exemplary family man.

The best matches for an Aquarius are female fellow Aquarians, Libras, and Sagittarians. When Aquarius seeks out yet another affair, he is not choosy, and will be happy with anyone.

PISCES

Pisces is the most eccentric sign of the Zodiac. This is reflected in his romantic tendencies and sex life. Pisces men become very dependent on those with whom they have a close relationship. Paradoxically, they are simultaneously crafty and childlike when it comes to playing games, and they are easily deceived. As a double bodied sign, Pisces rarely marry just once, as they are very sexual, easily fall in love, and are constantly seeking their ideal. Pisces are very warm people, who love to take care of others and are inclined toward "slave-master" relationships, in which they are the submissive partner. But after catering to so many lovers, Pisces will remain elusive. They are impossible to figure out ahead of time – today, they might be declaring their love for you, but tomorrow, they may disappear – possibly forever! To a Pisces, love is a fantasy, illusion, and dream, and they might spend their whole lives in pursuit of it. Pisces who are unhappy in love are vulnerable to alcoholism or drug addiction.

Cancer and Scorpio make the best partners for a Pisces. He is also easily dominated by Capricorn and Libra, but in turn will conquer even a queen-like Leo. Often, they are fascinated by Geminis – if they marry, it will last a long time, but likely not forever. Relationships with Aries and Sagittarians are erratic, though initially, things can seem almost perfect.

Women

ARIES

Aries women are leaders. They are decisive, bold, and very protective. An Aries can take initiative and is not afraid to make the first move. Her ideal man is strong, and someone she can admire. But remember, at the slightest whiff of weakness, she will knock him off his pedestal. She does not like dull, whiny men, and thinks that there is always a way out of any situation. If she loves someone, she will be faithful. Aries women are too honest to try leading a double life. They are possessive, jealous, and not only will they not forgive those who are unfaithful, their revenge may be brutal; they know no limits. If you can handle an Aries, don't try to put her in a cage; it is best to give her a long leash. Periodically give her some space – then she will seek you out herself. She is sexual, and believe that anything goes in bed.

Her best partners are a Sagittarius or Leo. A Libra can make a good match after middle age, once both partners have grown wiser and settled down a bit. Gemini and Aquarius are only good partners during the initial phase, when everything is still new, but soon enough, they will lose interest in each other. Scorpios are good matches in bed, but only suitable as lovers.

TAURUS

Taurean women possess qualities that men often dream about, but rarely find in the flesh – they are soft, charming, practical, and reliable – they are very caring and will support their partner in every way. A Taurus is highly sexual, affectionate, and can show a man how to take pleasure to new heights. She is also strong and intense. If she is in love, she will be faithful. But when love fades away, she might find someone else on the side, though she will still fight to save her marriage, particularly if her husband earns good money. A Taurus will not tolerate a man who is disheveled or disorganized, and anyone dating her needs to always be on his toes. She will expect gifts, and likes being taken to expensive restaurants, concerts, and other events. If you argue, try to make the first peace offering, because a Taurus finds it very hard to do so – she might withdraw and ruminate for a long time. Never air your dirty laundry; solve all your problems one-on-one.

Scorpio, Virgo, Capricorn, and Cancer make the best matches. A relationship with an Aries or Sagittarius would be difficult. There is little attraction between a Taurus and a Leo, and initially Libras can make for a good partner in bed, but things will quickly cool off and fall apart. A Taurus and Aquarius make an interesting match – despite the difference in signs, their relationships are often lasting, and almost lifelong.

GEMINI

Gemini women are social butterflies, outgoing, and they easily make friends, and then break off the friendship, if people do not hold their interest. A Gemini falls in love hard, is very creative, and often fantasizes about the object of her affection. She is uninterested in sex without any attachment, loves to flirt, and, for the most part, is not particularly affectionate. She dreams of a partner who is her friend, lover, and a romantic, all at once. A Gemini has no use for a man who brings nothing to the table intellectually. That is a tall order, so Geminis often divorce and marry several times. Others simply marry later in life. Once you have begun a life together, do not try to keep her inside – she needs to travel, explore, socialize, attend events and go to the theater. She cannot tolerate possessive men, so avoid giving her the third degree, and remember that despite her flirtatious and social nature, she is, in fact, faithful – as long as you keep her interested and she is in love. Astrologists believe that Geminis do not know what they need until age 29 or 30, so it is best to hold off on marriage until then.

Leo and Libra make the best matches. A relationship with a Cancer is likely, though complex, and depends solely on the Cancer's affection. A Gemini and Sagittarius can have an interesting, dynamic relationship, but these are two restless signs, which might only manage to get together after ages 40-45, once they have had enough thrills out of life and learned to be patient. Relationships with a Capricorn are very difficult, and almost never happen. The honeymoon stage can be wonderful with a Scorpio, but each partner will eventually go their own way, before ending things. A Gemini and Pisces union can also be very interesting – they are drawn to each other, and can have a wonderful relationship, but after a while, the cracks start to show and things will fall apart. An Aquarius is also not a bad match, but they will have little sexual chemistry.

CANCER

Cancers can be divided into two opposing groups. The first includes a sweet and gentle creature who is willing to dedicate her life to her husband and children. She is endlessly devoted to her husband, especially if he makes a decent living and remains faithful. She views all men as potential husbands, which means it is dangerous to strike up a relationship with her if your intentions are not serious; she can be anxious and clingy, sensitive and prone to crying. It is better to break things to her gently, rather than directly spitting out the cold, hard truth. She wants a man who can be a provider, though she often earns well herself. She puts money away for a rainy day, and knows how to be thrifty, for the sake of others around her, rather than only for herself. She is an excellent cook and capable of building an inviting home for her loved ones. She is enthusiastic in bed, a wonderful wife, and a caring mother.

The second type of Cancer is neurotic, and capable of creating a living hell for those around her. She believes that the world is her enemy, and manages to constantly find new intrigue and machinations.

Another Cancer, Virgo, Taurus, Scorpio, and Pisces make the best matches. A Cancer can often fall in love with a Gemini, but eventually, things will grow complicated, as she will be exhausted by a Gemini's constant mood swings and cheating. A Cancer and Sagittarius will initially have passionate sex, but things will quickly cool off. A relationship with a Capricorn is a real possibility, but only later in life, as while they are young, they are likely to fight and argue constantly. Cancer can also have a relationship with an Aries, but this will not be easy.

LEO

Leos are usually beautiful or charming, and outwardly sexual. And yet, appearances can be deceiving – they are not actually that interested in sex. Leo women want to be the center of attention and men running after them boosts their self-esteem, but they are more interested in their career, creating something new, and success than sex. They often have high-powered careers and are proud of their own achievements. Their partners need to be strong; if a Leo feels a man is weak, she can carry him herself for a while- before leaving him. It is difficult for her to find a partner for life, as chivalrous knights are a dying breed, and she is not willing to compromise. If you are interested in a Leo, take the initiative, admire her, and remember that even a queen is still a woman. Timid men or tightwads need not apply. Leos like to help others, but they don't need a walking disaster in their life. If they are married and in love, they are usually faithful, and petty gossip isn't their thing. Leo women make excellent mothers, and are ready to give their lives to their children. Their negative traits include vanity and a willingness to lie, in order to make themselves look better.

Sagittarius, Aries, and Libra make the best matches. Leos can also have an interesting relationship with a Virgo, though both partners will weaken each other. Life with a Taurus will lead to endless arguments – both signs are very stubborn, and unwilling to give in. Leos and Pisces are another difficult pair, as she will have to learn to be submissive if she wants to keep him around. A relationship with a Capricorn will work if there is a common denominator, but they will have little sexual chemistry. Life with a Scorpio will be turbulent to say the least, and they will usually break up later in life.

VIRGO

Virgo women are practical, clever, and often duplicitous. Marrying one isn't for everyone. She is a neat freak to the point of annoying those around her. She is also an excellent cook, and strives to ensure her children receive the very best by teaching them everything, and preparing them for a bright future. She is also thrifty – she won't throw money around, and, in fact, won't even give it to her husband. She has no time for rude, macho strongmen, and is suspicious of spendthrifts. She will not be offended if you take her to a cozy and modest café rather than an elegant restaurant. Virgos are masters of intrigue, and manage to outperform every other sign of the Zodiac in this regard. Virgos love to criticize everyone and everything; to listen to them, the entire world is simply a disaster and wrong, and only she is the exception to this rule. Virgos are not believed to be particularly sexual, but there are different variations when it comes to this. Rarely, one finds an open-minded Virgo willing to try anything, and who does it all on a grand scale – but she is rather the exception to this general rule.

The best matches for a Virgo are Cancer, Taurus, and Capricorn. She also can get along well with a Scorpio, but will find conflict with Sagittarius. A Pisces will strike her interest, but they will rarely make it down the aisle. She is often attracted to an Aquarius, but they would drive each other up the wall were they to actually marry. An Aries forces Virgo to see another side of life, but here, she will have to learn to conform and adapt.

LIBRA

Female Libras tend to be beautiful, glamorous, or very charming. They are practical, tactical, rational, though they are adept at hiding these qualities behind their romantic and elegant appearance. Libras are drawn to marriage, and are good at imagining the kind of partner they need. They seek out strong, well-off men and are often more interested in someone's social status and bank account than feelings. The object of their affection needs to be dashing, and have a good reputation in society. Libras love expensive things, jewelry, and finery. If they are feeling down, a beautiful gift will instantly cheer them up. They will not tolerate scandal or conflict, and will spend all their energy trying to keep the peace, or at least the appearance thereof. They do not like to air their dirty laundry, and will only divorce in extreme circumstances. They are always convinced they are right and react to any objections as though they have been insulted. Most Libras are not particularly sexual, except those with Venus or the Moon in Scorpio.

Leos, Geminis, and Aquarians make good matches. Libra women are highly attracted to Aries men - this is a real case of opposites attract. They can get along with a Sagittarius, though he will find that Libras are too proper and calm. Capricorn, Pisces, and Cancer are all difficult matches. Things will begin tumultuously with a Taurus, before each partner goes his or her own way.

SCORPIO

Scorpio women may appear outwardly restrained, but there is much more bubbling below the surface. They are ambitious with high self-esteem, but often wear a mask of unpretentiousness. They are the true power behind the scenes, the one who holds the family together, but never talk about it. Scorpios are strong-willed, resilient, and natural survivors. Often, Scorpios are brutally honest, and expect the same out of those around them. They do not like having to conform, and attempt to get others to adapt to them, as they honestly believe everyone will be better off that way. They are incredibly intuitive, and not easily deceived. They have an excellent memory, and can quickly figure out which of your buttons to push. They are passionate in bed, and their temperament will not diminish with age. When she is sexually frustrated, a Scorpio will throw all of her energy into her career or her loved ones. She is proud, categorical, and "if you don't do it right, don't do it at all" is her motto. Scorpio cannot be fooled, and she will not forgive any cheating. Will she cheat herself? Yes! But it will not break up her family, and she will attempt to keep it a secret. Scorpios are usually attractive to men, even if they are not particularly beautiful. They keep a low profile, though they always figure out their partner, and give them some invisible sign. There is also another, selfish type of Scorpio, who will use others for as long as they need them, before unceremoniously casting them aside.

Taurus is a good match; they will have excellent sexual chemistry and understand each other. Scorpio and Gemini are drawn to each other, but are unlikely to stay together long enough to actually get married. Cancer can be a good partner as well, but Cancers are possessive, while Scorpios do not like others meddling in their affairs, though they can later resolve their arguments in bed. Scorpio and Leo are often found together, but their relationship can also be very complicated. Leos are animated and chipper, while Scorpios, who are much deeper and more stubborn, see Leos as not particularly serious or reliable. One good example of this is Bill (a Leo) and Hillary (a Scorpio) Clinton. Virgo can also make a good partner, but when Scorpio seemingly lacks emotions, he will look for them elsewhere. Relationships with Lira are strange and very rare. Scorpio sees Libra as too insecure, and Libra does not appreciate Scorpio's rigidity. Two Scorpios together make an excellent marriage! Sagittarius and Scorpio are unlikely to get together, as she will think he is shallow and rude. If they do manage to get married, Scorpio's drive and persistence is the only thing that will make the marriage last. Capricorn is also not a bad match, and while Scorpio finds Aquarius attractive, they will rarely get married, as they are simply speaking different languages! Things are alright with a Pisces, as both signs are emotional, and Pisces can let Scorpio take the lead when necessary.

SAGITTARIUS

Sagittarius women are usually charming, bubbly, energetic, and have the gift of gab. They are kind, sincere, and love people. They are also straightforward, fair, and very ambitious, occasionally to the point of irritating those around them. But telling them something is easier than not telling them, and they often manage to win over their enemies. Sagittarius tends to have excellent intuition, and she loves to both learn and teach others. She is a natural leader, and loves taking charge at work and at home. Many Sagittarian women have itchy feet, and prefer all kinds of travel to sitting at home. They are not particularly good housewives – to be frank, cooking and cleaning is simply not for them. Their loved ones must learn to adapt to them, but Sagittarians themselves hate any pressure. They are not easy for men to handle, as Sagittarians want to be in charge. Sagittarius falls in love easily, is very sexual and temperamental, and may marry multiple times. Despite outward appearances, Sagittarius is a very lonely sign. Even after she is married with children, she may continue living as if she were alone; you might say she marches to the beat of her own drum. Younger

Sagittarians can be reckless, but as they mature, they can be drawn to religion, philosophy, and the occult.

Aries and Leo make the best matches, as Sagittarius is able to bend to Leo's ways, or at least pretend to. Sagittarians often end up with Aquarians, but their marriages do not tend to be for the long haul. They are attracted to Geminis, but are unlikely to marry one until middle age, when both signs have settled down. Sagittarius and Cancer have incredible sexual chemistry, but an actual relationship between them would be tumultuous and difficult. Capricorn can make a good partner- as long as they are able to respect each other's quirks. Sagittarius rarely ends up with a Virgo, and while she may often meet Pisces, things are unlikely to go very far.

CAPRICORN

Capricorn women are conscientious, reliable, organized, and hard-working. Many believe that life means nothing but work, and live accordingly. They are practical, and not particularly drawn to parties or loud groups of people. But if someone useful will be there, they are sure to make an appearance. Capricorn women are stingy, but not as much as their male counterparts. They are critical of others, but think highly of themselves. Generally, they take a difficult path in life, but thanks to their dedication, perseverance, and willingness to push their own limits, they are able to forge their own path, and by 45 or 50, they can provide themselves with anything they could want. Capricorn women have the peculiarity of looking older than their peers when they are young, and younger than everyone else once they have matured. They are not particularly sexual, and tend to be faithful partners. They rarely divorce, and even will fight until the end, even for a failed marriage. Many Capricorns have a pessimistic outlook of life, and have a tendency to be depressed. They are rarely at the center of any social circle, but are excellent organizers. They have a very rigid view of life and love, and are not interested in a fling, as marriage is the end goal. As a wife, Capricorn is simultaneously difficult and reliable. She is difficult because of her strict nature and difficulty adapting. But she will also take on all the household duties, and her husband can relax, knowing his children are in good hands.

Taurus, Pisces, and Scorpio make good matches. Aries is difficult, once things cool off after the initial honeymoon. When a Capricorn meets another Capricorn, they will be each other's first and last love. Sagittarius isn't a bad match, but they don't always pass the test of time. Aquarius and Capricorn are a difficult match, and rarely found together. Things are too dull with a Virgo, and while Leo can be exciting at first, things will fall apart when he begins showing off. Libra and Aquarius are both difficult partners for Capricorn, and she is rarely found with either of them.

AQUARIUS

A female Aquarius is very different from her male counterparts. She is calm and keeps a cool head, but she is also affectionate and open. She values loyalty above all else, and is unlikely to recover from any infidelity, though she will only divorce if this becomes a chronic trend, and she has truly been stabbed in the back. She is not interested in her partner's money, but rather, his professional success. She is unobtrusive and trusting, and will refrain from listening in on her partner's phone conversations or hacking into his email. With rare exceptions, Aquarian women make terrible housewives. But they are excellent partners in life – they are faithful, never boring, and will not reject a man, even in the most difficult circumstances. Most Aquarians are highly intuitive, and can easily tell the truth from a lie. They themselves only lie in extreme situations, which call for a "white lie" in order to avoid hurting someone's feelings.

Aquarius gets along well with Aries, Gemini, and Libra. She can also have a good relationship with a Sagittarius. Taurus often makes a successful match, though they are emotionally very different; the same goes for Virgo. Aquarius and Scorpio, Capricorn, or Cancer is a difficult match. Pisces can make a good partner as well, as both signs complement each other. Any relationship with a Leo will be tumultuous, but lasting, as Leo is selfish, and Aquarius will therefore have to be very forgiving.

PISCES

Pisces women are very adaptable, musically inclined, and erotic. They possess an innate earthly wisdom, and a good business sense. Pisces often reinvent themselves; they can be emotional, soft, and obstinate, as well as sentimental, at times. Their behavioral changes can be explained by frequent ups and downs. Pisces is charming, caring, and her outward malleability is very attractive to men. She is capable of loving selflessly, as long as the man has something to love. Even if he doesn't, she will try and take care of him until the very end. Pisces' greatest fear is poverty. They are intuitive, vulnerable, and always try to avoid conflict. They love to embellish the truth, and sometimes alcohol helps with this. Rarely, one finds extremely unbalanced, neurotic and dishonest Pisces, who are capable of turning their loved ones' lives into a living Hell!

Taurus, Capricorn, Cancer, and Scorpio make the best matches. She will be greatly attracted to a Virgo, but a lasting relationship is only likely if both partners are highly spiritual. Any union with a Libra is likely to be difficult and full of conflict. Pisces finds Gemini attractive, and they may have a very lively relationship – for a while. Occasionally, Pisces ends up with a Sagittarius, but she will have to fade into the background and entirely submit to him. If she ends up with an Aquarius, expect strong emotional outbursts, and a marriage that revolves around the need to raise their children.

Tatiana Borsch

Printed in France by Amazon
Brétigny-sur-Orge, FR